THE edition of this book is limited to 120 copies printed on hand-made paper, autographed by Madame Thamar Karsavina, with all the decorations coloured by hand, numbered 1 to 120.
And 230 copies printed on antique paper, numbered 121 to 350.

THAMAR KARSAVINA

THAMAR KARSAVINA

By
VALERIEN SVETLOV

Translated from the Russian by
H. DE VERE BEAUCLERK & NADIA EVRENOV

Edited by
CYRIL W. BEAUMONT

1922
LONDON
C. W. BEAUMONT
75 CHARING CROSS ROAD W.C. 2

First published in 1922

This facsimile edition published in 2019 by

The Noverre Press
Southwold House
Isington Road
Binsted
Hampshire
GU34 4PH

© 2019 The Noverre Press

EDITOR'S NOTE

I DESIRE to express my appreciation of the valuable assistance rendered to me in the editing of this book by my friends E. Powys Mathers and E. F. Escott, while in the colouring of the decorations in the special edition I desire to record the kindly collaboration of Mrs. Claude Lovat Fraser in the preparation of the colour schemes, a proceeding rendered necessary by the sudden death of her gifted husband.

CYRIL W. BEAUMONT

CONTENTS

	PAGE
Introduction	1
Prelude	5
First Steps	9
Searchings	23
The Path of Fame	37
Ten Years	68
The Height	74
Conclusions	93
Bibliography	137
The Ballet Répertoire of Thamar Karsavina	139
Index of Names, Rôles and Ballets	145

TABLE OF DRAWINGS

FACING PAGE

T. Karsavina in *Thamar*, from the painting by Glyn Philpot, A.R.A. . . . . *Frontispiece*

T. Karsavina, from the drawing by V. Seroff 12

Design for *The Two Blackbirds* (Mme. Karsavina's costume), by Claude Lovat Fraser 18

T. Karsavina, from the drawing by John J. Sargent, R.A. . . 24

T. Karsavina in *Petrouchka*, from the statue by Soudbinin . . 30

T. Karsavina in *Les Sylphides*, from the drawing by Randolph Schwabe 38

T. Karsavina in *Le Spectre de la Rose*, from the drawing by Randolph Schwabe 44

T. Karsavina in *Le Carnaval*, from the drawing by Randolph Schwabe 48

First Sketch for the costume of the Queen of Shemåkhan in *Le Coq d'Or*, by Natalie Gontcharova 54

T. Karsavina in *Schéhérazade*, from drawing by Randolph Schwabe 60

T. Karsavina in *Le Dieu Bleu*, from the drawing by L. Kainer. . 64

T. Karsavina in *Petrouchka*, from the drawing by Adrian P. Allinson 70

T. Karsavina in *Giselle*, from the statue by Soudbinin . . . 76

T. Karsavina in *The Three Cornered Hat*, from the drawing by Randolph Schwabe 82

T. Karsavina in *Le Astuzie Femminili*, from the drawing by Randolph Schwabe 90

T. Karsavina in her Dressing Room, from the drawing by Randolph Schwabe 96

T. Karsavina in *The Good Humoured Ladies*, from the drawing by Adrian P. Allinson 100

The text decorated by Claude Lovat Fraser. The cover, preliminary pages and p. 103 decorated by Randolph Schwabe.

TABLE OF CAMERA PORTRAITS

	PAGE
Rôle of Giselle in *Giselle*	107
Rôle of Zobeide in *Schéhérazade*	109
Rôle of Columbine in *Le Carnaval*	111
Rôle of Armide in *Le Pavillon d'Armide*	113
Rôle of the Queen of Shemåkhan in *Le Coq d'Or*	115
Rôle of Sylphide in *Les Sylphides*	117
Rôle of the Young Girl in *Papillons*	119
Rôle of the Maiden in *Le Spectre de la Rose*	121
Rôle of Chloë in *Daphnis et Chloë*	123
Rôle of the Ballerine in *Petrouchka*	125
Rôle of Salome in *The Tragedy of Salome*	127
Rôle of the Fire-Bird in *L'Oiseau de Feu*	129
Rôle of the Miller's Wife in *The Three Cornered Hat*	131
Rôle of Pimpinella in *Pulcinella*	133
Pas de Deux in *Le Astuzie Femminili*	135

INTRODUCTION

IT is only of late that the ballet has begun to be appreciated by the general public [1] and thus become a regular subject for criticism. For many years it had existed humbly among other dramatic arts; the *maîtres-de-ballet* adhering to the hard and fast traditions bequeathed to them by the French classical school ... added to this, a succession of Italian dancers, male and female, set the fashion on the Imperial stage of a highly exaggerated technique. The ballet was supported by a mere handful of faithful ballet lovers. The public in general was supremely indifferent to it; while criticism accorded but an occasional and half-disdainful attention.

Diaghileff and Fokine wrought a complete change. Traditions were thrown overboard and the ballet rose from the depths in which it had been sinking. The interests both of audiences and critics in this new departure grew steadily. Nevertheless ballet criticism was still limited to brief notices of the performance; it concerned itself solely with the personal success of the dancers and the bouquets they received. Now together with the renaissance of the ballet, there arose a more lively curiosity in respect of the choregraphic art. The curt notices developed into critical reviews, and later into books. ...

The ballet presents a too specialised art for any one with merely ordinary knowledge of the subject to write about it. To throw off a newspaper report, as was done until quite recently, is easy. A short account of the performance or performances, with

[1] In Russia.

a sprinkling of technical terms, may give an ignorant public the impression that it has been written by an expert. At the same time, a scientifically detailed article written by a *real* expert who has studied thoroughly the technique of dancing, does not appear to be the exact criticism people require. Every one interested in choregraphy, whether as art or spectacle, will always prefer something written by a lover of the beautiful—a genuine admirer of the art he describes. Such an article pleases the reader and appeals to the artist. The public does not understand technical terms; the dancers know them better than any critic. A review of the ballet must be written by an artist—I mean by some one who appreciates art—and whose passionate criticism is capable of moving the reader and inspiring him to love an art he sincerely loves himself. All other criticism is worthless.

Again, it is, of course, easy to make a statement concerning a dancer's capabilities. The dancer has executed such and such *adagios*, *variations*, *pas de deux*. I have read detailed descriptions of *variations*, technical enumerations of every movement, every step, every position, but this is not an artistic form of criticism; rather is it a photographic film conveying no artistic impressions of plastic movement or attitude whatsoever. An *artist* would have known how to render effective the impressions he received, for as they passed through his imagination they would have inspired him with thoughts and words far different from a commonplace list of the steps composing the dance. In brief, a criticism to be of value must be neither notice nor photograph of a dramatic performance; it must be a literary work having its own artistic merit. . . .

Not every portrait painter is an artist; nor is every portrait a work of art. A portrait may be a striking likeness; may render with wonderful wealth of technique every detail of flesh and costume. Yet it may be merely a coloured photograph. It is only when the painter succeeds in revealing the spirit of the original —when he is able by means of concrete drawing and material accessories to make the soul felt beneath the technique of line, light and shadow; to transmit the charm and admiration he himself feels—that the portrait, instead of being the soulless photograph taken by an experienced craftsman, becomes the priceless work of a poet-artist.

Karsavina is a dancer of the Russian renaissance of the ballet endowed with new life by the combined efforts of *maîtres-de-ballet*, artists, composers and dancers, united by Diaghileff's inspired and persistent initiative. He has brought about the revolution of the Russian ballet on the stages of Paris and London, overthrowing everywhere the regime of a dying plastic art.

Karsavina is the world-famed name of the *première danseuse* of the new Russian ballet. The *maîtres-de-ballet* Fokine, Nijinsky and Romanoff have collaborated with her; likewise the painters Alexander Benois, Roehrich, Seroff, Bakst, Doboujinsky, Souroff, Soudeikine, and the composers Glazounoff, Stravinsky, Tcherepnine, Debussy and Dukas.... She has inspired a wide literature and possesses an iconography to herself. Her artistic grace and inspired plastic attitudes have given vitality to the visions of these creators of the modern Russian ballet. Hers has been the dramatic genius appearing in poems and colours, melody and rhythm. She has evolved a series of images of dramatic force, lyrical tenderness, and plastic beauty. Her fascinating art of mime and the rhythm of her dancing have recalled Russian fairy-tales, ancient myths, romantic dreams....

To write the life-story of Karsavina, one must be able to represent her true artistic image and to reveal her artist soul. That is the only criticism possible of her life *en scène*.

It might have been easier to write a book about the great dancer without this Introduction, which must of a necessity beget certain expectations. I may not be able to attain the high standard I have set myself. I can only say I have addressed myself to the task with a deep and genuine affection for the art that all my life has enthralled my senses—also with a feeling of deep admiration for the dancer's wonderful gifts. It is not for me to judge whether I have rightly understood the artistic substance underlying her rare talents or whether I have succeeded in imparting to others the thrill of delight her art has given me....

PRELUDE

KARSAVINA ...

TO me the name recalls images of bygone Hellas. In a sacred laurel grove are the marble columns of an ancient temple, where before fragrant altars dance rose-crowned maidens. One of their number is clad in a snow-white tunic. She is slender; in every movement, graceful. On her beautiful and classic features the sadness lingers of the goddess descended to earth from the crimson radiance of Olympus, home of eternal happiness and of hymns sung evermore to Joy and Beauty. The maiden seeks the reflection of these delights among men, and is transformed into the nymph Echo,[1] her translucent raiment dyed to the hue of mournful purple. Thus she wanders, sad and forgotten, through the valleys of Hellas. Thus she roams in wild gorges, between red rocks, by singing streams, beneath the shade of olive groves: ever seeking her lost dream, her unforgettable ideal.

For an instant she believes it found in fair, curly-haired Narcissus; but deception soon follows, and once again the nymph is left alone with her ancient grief; her sighs and lamentations echo amidst the valleys, gorges, and woods. ...

THAMAR ...

The mere sound of the name brings visions of the Orient, thrilling in their strangeness and unrevealed mystery.

[1] Karsavina's *rôle* in the ballet *Narcisse*.

On the deep-piled carpets of the *harêm*, upon soft cushions, recline idle *odalisques* and singing-girls. Among them glide pale-faced eunuchs—passionless ghosts, indifferent to the white bodies recumbent on Eastern tissues; their eyes ungladdened by the sumptuous tints that reflect all the colours of the sunbeam.

From a shadowy garden, visible through the curiously fretted tracery of arches, the sound floats of music, now subdued, now fiercely passionate. The Shah's beloved favourite lies dreaming, her lithe form coiled luxuriously upon the cushions of the *diwân*.

No blood tinges her cheek. Her face is pallid. No gleam lurks in her eyes, dark as a moonless night. Even the thoughts of this Scheherazade seem to sleep, and her heart to beat no more. Yet beneath this immobility there gathers a violent storm.

Her brain conceives plans of treachery; her heart throbs with a guilty passion for the handsome slave. The climax of the drama draws near. The hour of Oriental tragedy is imminent. . . .

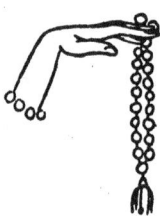

AN image of Hellas and a vision of the East—they are not the only plastic and choregraphic creations of Thamar Karsavina. Hellas drew its culture from the East, and there exists in the history of Greece a period when it is difficult to separate the evidences of Eastern civilisation from those of the secular Hellenic spirit. Although centuries have passed, traces of Helleno-Asiaticism still linger in the modern intelligence; still live and breathe under the deep stratum of European cultivation; strange if it did not live in the soul of Karsavina—Greek by descent. The images she evokes in *Narcisse* and *Schéhérazade* are among the most fascinating of Oriental Hellenism.

The myths of ancient classic times endure for ever. The important part played in them by metamorphosis is well known. Narcissus is changed into a flower; the nymph Echo into a rock, to repeat plaintively the sounds of the human voice. These transformations are the effect of reincarnation into successive images—a gift of transposition possessed only by artistic natures. It would be impossible to enumerate all Karsavina's reincarnations.

I remember her as a sylphide-spirit in the romantic night of Chopin. I remember her as a weird wraith in mystic moonlight. I remember her in the dread kingdom of the *Ghosts*, transformed from the tortured *ballerina* into a winged phantom. Now she is the beautiful enchantress *Armide*, whom the wizard-marquis summons to destroy *Réné de Beaugency*. Now, again, she is the innocent young girl in a muslin room who dreams of her love for a rose; while as *Ta-Hor* she falls in anguish over the prostrate body of a man who has spurned her faithful love for the sake of a fleeting passion for a soulless Cleopatra. By the shores of the strange lake of the Swans she is subjected to the spell of the devil Rotbart, to satisfy Siegfried's love. In the radiance of Botticelli's garden she is the ethereal spirit of the *Preludes*. She enacts sentimental *Columbine* and the 1830 naïve child by whom poor Pierrot is so mischievously tricked. She becomes the cunning *Kitri*, who deceives her father, the innkeeper, in the small Spanish inn set below the twinkling lights of many-coloured lanterns and a shower of falling flowers. . . .

It is not necessary to specify all the images, the fairy tales, the legends, the myths, in which Thamar Karsavina has been made incarnate. She is the Queen of a wondrous fairy art; the priestess of metempsychosis. She gathers the beauty dispersed about the world and gives vivid form to half-felt thoughts and hidden dreams.

It is for that we honour this weaver of golden dream-threads. . . .

FIRST STEPS

IN 1902 Karsavina made her first steps in our ballet school, when it bore the title of *St. Petersburg and Imperial*. Now it bears that of the *Petrograd State*.

The director of Crown theatres at that earlier time was V. A. Teliakovsky, and it was under his management that the displays of ballet pupils finishing at the school were first opened to the public. Before that, in the time of T. A. Vsevolojsky, the public were not usually admitted to the performances. On the completion of their training, the pupils underwent examination in a strictly academic atmosphere. The successful candidates were permitted to take part in a public performance, five or six months later, on the regular stage, where they were lost among the throng of the *corps de ballet*. Here the *coryphées* were so numerous that it was as much out of the question to judge adequately the talents of the neophytes as to criticise the art and resources of their teachers. Again, for the aspirants to distinguish themselves from the crowd and show personality in important groups on a large stage took considerable time; whereas the test system of public displays produced at once a group of young *figurantes* whose dancing gave an approximate idea, not only of their several degrees of native talent, but also of the adequacy of their respective schools of professional training. I say an approximate idea advisedly, because at a first public appearance it is common for even an experienced critic greatly to misjudge a beginner. For some time before the decisive day the pupils undergo a very serious preparation. A small ballet, with a *divertissement*, is chosen and rehearsals continue until it is perfectly mastered by the girls. These rehearsals are pursued so rigorously that, in the case of a pupil who has done her task well and conscientiously grappled with the prescribed *variations*, it needs an extremely keen sense of ballet criticism, besides an infinity of experience, to discriminate between the true natural gift and the purely mechanical results of hard study. On the other hand, a pupil may be found unsatisfactory, either in her *rôle* or in the *variations*, simply on account of a momentary nervousness or a sudden fit of depression. It is not easy to determine justly when a pupil's performance is influenced by so many factors. A wealth of experience and minute attention are required to give so many considerations and conditions their true value. Perhaps the simplest element to estimate is the style and system which the professor has required of his students; that is to say, the correct pose of the body, arms, and feet, the degrees of plastic expression, freedom of movement, and so on. . . .

It is quite true that a few artistic natures exhibit their natural gifts so clearly from the first that no one can possibly be mistaken as to their aptitude. It is of little account how such a pupil dances at the examination or how many technical mistakes she makes: the spectator or critic, however discerning he may be in regard to wrong movements, cannot help feeling that, in seeing her, he sees a truly artistic personality.

Genius, that great Something which no one has ever yet been able to define, produces light and warmth; diffuses itself into a myriad radiant hues, eclipsing all imperfections and unmastered mechanical efforts.

Such rarely gifted natures were Anna Pavlova and Thamar Karsavina. Sparks of their genius already glimmer on the examination boards, then more or less quickly burst into flame. They leave a deep impression on the history of art, and are crowned with the diadem of the great exponents of choregraphy.

From the beginning Pavlova's talent blazed like a great fire—a dazzling meteor, she gleamed across our stage and those of Europe and America.

The talent of Thamar Karsavina developed more slowly. It flowered brightly at her *début* on the large stage in autumn, then it seemed to fade, as though in misgiving—as if endeavouring to test itself—while observing its own nature and the strength of its powers of artistic creation.

For a long while Karsavina seemed to be searching for herself, to be watching with torturing doubt for some real proof of the genius she felt stirring within her. But she seemed to fear it, to wish to restrain it, lest it should prove spurious. This period of probation was not brief. Perhaps it was from these misgivings, hopes, fears, and struggles—all painful for the artist—that came the great talent that made of Karsavina the first dancer in Europe.

TO return to the display on March 22nd, 1902. This *Performance of the Pupils of the St. Petersburg Imperial Schools*, as it was called, took place at the Michel Theatre. Two classes were examined, one of P. A. Gerdt, the other of R. M. Kulichevskaïa.

Thamar Karsavina 'finished' in P. A. Gerdt's class. She was awarded the white dress[1] and received the maximum number of marks for her dancing. Here I should mention that, while still a pupil, Karsavina was considered highly gifted. Serious parts had been allotted to her even before the examinations. At the 'Chinese Theatre' of Tsarkoe Selo she had accomplished a difficult and important *rôle* from the ballet of *Le Lac des Cygnes*, with T. A. Sedova and Obukhoff.

A short one-act ballet, almost devoid of dramatic interest, was chosen for the examination. It was called *In the Kingdom of Ice*. The music was written by members of the ballet who preserved their anonymity under the initials T. C. and P. M. The professor himself staged the production.

Simple music, an insignificant dramatic interest, with dances

[1] Three differently coloured dresses were worn in class, the colour serving to mark the pupil's progress. *Grey* was for the lowest, then *pink*, and *white* for the highest. The maximum number of marks was 12. It is interesting to note that Karsavina's professor emphasised his opinion of her dancing by marking her 12 +.

to correspond, were calculated almost completely to obscure the natural gifts of the pupils. Again, the absence of drama afforded no opportunity for the young beginners to display their knowledge of the art of mime. Finally, the primitive rhythm of the music prevented any judgment from being formed as to the dancer's ear for music.

Yet, as soon as Karsavina appeared in the *adagio*, a whisper of admiration passed through the audience. She did not appear alone. L. Kyasht had completed her school training at the same time, and for a long while afterwards was considered her rival on the stage of the *Mariynsky Theatre*. This serves to show how difficult it is to estimate the talent of a young artist.

The principals in the ballet were the pupil Monakhoff, who played the *rôle* of the *Young Hunter*, the pupil Andrianoff, since dead, who took the part of the *King of the Alpine Ice*, and Karsavina and Kyasht, who were the two *Snowflakes*. The dancing consisted of an *ensemble*, an *adagio* for the two *débutantes*, and for each, one *variation*. Between these were groups which represented snow-eddies, gnomes, and the fog. In addition to the dances mentioned there were six small *variations* for the other pupils under examination, including those who had not been previously presented. The ballet ended, according to custom, with a general *finale*.

Everything was exceedingly simple and primitive. To display personality in such a traditionally mediocre ballet scheme was impossible. What was visible was merely that which could not be concealed—the plastic beauty of the body and the knowledge of the principles of the classic school, that is to say, the pose of the figure, the position of the feet, and the carriage of the arms.

Both the pupils under examination were endowed with these externals, so essential to the choreographic art. The youthful Karsavina was the symbol of a spring night, for her pale face was framed in her black hair, and she had pensive beauty in her dark, visionary eyes.

And beside her was Kyasht—young as she—rosy and fair-haired, with laughing blue eyes, a finely built body, tending just perceptibly to plumpness; bright, gay, and active—a real spring day, without secrets or regrets, beckoning to the feast of life and the joy of living.

In the good old days, authors loved such extremes. If one

heroine was dark-haired and melancholy, the other had to be golden-haired and merry. It is always the story of Tatiana and Olga.[1] And such, indeed, were the two rivals and *débutantes* of 1902.

Their dancing betrayed at once the characteristics of their respective temperaments. Self-confidence showed itself already in that of Lydia Kyasht. She danced gaily, sprang high and lightly. Her performance had coquetry and grace. The conclusions of her *variations*, her gestures and movements, were impulsive. She seemed to be hurrying, eager. . . .

Thamar Karsavina, on the contrary, displayed the study of classic technique. In so young a dancer, the grace of her attitudes was unusual. Her gestures and movements were soft, rounded, plastic and noble. She revealed a remarkable understanding of the rhythm of motion. Real poetry emanated from her dancing, which resembled an elegy sung in the twilight by a voice hushed with emotion.

This is a fair definition of the two dancers' powers. Both were accepted on the stage after the trial performance. The rivals divided the public into two camps, each with reliance on 'its' dancer.

KARSAVINA'S first appearance at the *Mariynsky Theatre* was in the spring, on the last day of the closing season. She was let out of school on an 'increased salary' of sixty roubles a month (£6).

This is what the dancer herself says about her first appearance in her *Recollections*, published in the magazine *Je sais tout* (November 15th, 1912, No. 31):—

[1] Characters from Poushkin's poem *Eugene Oneguin*.

'Soon I shall have been nine years on the stage, but I remember well the night of my first appearance. I took part in a *pas de deux* introduced into the last act of the ballet *Javotte*. It was an old *pas de deux*, danced once upon a time by Zucchi, and called *The Fisherman and the Pearl*. I did not experience any fear, but I was in an excitable mood, and I longed to hasten the moment of my appearance on the stage. I was almost certain of my success, and the agitation I felt was pleasant. At the present time I am far more exacting than I was then, and I am, therefore, far more nervous than I was at the moment when my fate was decided. Now it seems to me that I never have had such a great success— and that first year was a series of easy successes. Towards the end of the season I appeared in the capacity of *première danseuse* in the one-act ballet *Le Réveil de Flore*.'

'K. A. Skalkovsky,' continues Karsavina in her *Recollections*, 'a clever man and an expert in dancing, spoke pleasantly of my *début*.' Having praised the young and promising dancer's attitudes, he added that by her origin she belonged to a great people, who have given birth to gods and heroes, but whose descendants are obliged now to sell sponges and Turkish delight. 'In order to follow his meaning, it must be remembered that my grandmother was a Greek.'

After the summer holidays, the young dancer appeared again at the *Mariynsky Theatre*.

Variations, which were small, but important for a beginner, were given her in the *Golden Waltz* of *Casse-Noisette* and in *Javotte*. Lastly, she danced one of the three well-known *variations* in the *Ghosts* of *La Bayadère*.

The two other *variations* in that motif were danced by two already well-known dancers, V. A. Trefilova and V. T. Rykliakova.

FOLLOWING upon this successful opening, the dancer's career seemed to come suddenly to a standstill. It was as though something untoward had happened to the young artist, a crisis in her fate, a loss of faith in her future, a state of depression. She appeared to take less pains to develop her youthful and promising abilities; while a certain degree of carelessness and an absence of energy were noticeable in her dancing. It was a painful epoch in Karsavina's life, and contrasted unfavourably with her artistic *début*.

In the *Recollections*—already mentioned—she refers to that period in the following words: ' Off the stage I had a very good time, and enjoyed perfect freedom and independence. Balls and parties followed charity bazaars, and I was so fascinated and carried away by the pleasures of this new existence, that I would often miss the lessons of my old dancing master, Johannsen, for which he scolded me. In particular, he strictly forbade me to dance at parties—remarking that such dancing weakens the feet. However, I soon understood how imperative it was for me to renew my studies. I was no longer being called enthusiastically before the curtain; no longer being noisily acclaimed by the pit, as I had been during my first appearances, even when I failed to make the right steps or *pirouette*, or when my legs grew heavy with weakness.

' For some time I felt a distinct coldness on the part of the public for my performances on the stage, and, naturally, this was very distressing to me. I, too, realised that I had lost some of my former strength and precision. So, taking advantage of leave of absence, I went to Italy in order to study under Signora Beretta, celebrated as a professor of classical dancing.'

In the summer of 1903 Karsavina fell grievously sick, and was prevented by a long illness and subsequent weakness from appearing on the stage at the beginning of the autumn season.

' I went to Milan,' she continues in her memoirs, ' in the autumn of 1903. I was exceedingly weak. Towards the end of the first lesson at Signora Beretta's I felt faint, and swooned. I must say that the Italian exercises were far longer than those to which I had been accustomed.'

The dancer's recollections of the teacher who ' set her on her feet ' were of the kindliest.

' The strength I so suddenly lost,' Karsavina proceeds,

' gradually returned to me. A year later, in the autumn, I again went to Signora Beretta's. She was quite a dear, and such a funny creature. Once upon a time she had been famous for the strength and precision of her dancing. Now, she was a small, fat woman, and almost a pauper. She never rose from her armchair to show me a movement or a position. Always feeling cold, she wrapped herself in a shawl; and often in the middle of a lesson would ask her old servant, Marcella, to rub her feet and cover them with a rug. Marcella was general servant and the friend of all. She would do anything; make the tunics, run errands, and prepare the vermouth which several of Signora Beretta's pupils were in the habit of drinking after lessons. Signora Beretta was most imposing to look at. She usually carried a stick, with which she beat time, and when the lesson was over, we kissed her hand and she kissed our foreheads. Her big feet rested on a red velvet cushion, and she looked like an old queen.'

IT would not be out of place to say here a few words about the teachers who gave a special lustre, a special finish and direction, to the celebrated dancer's natural gifts.

At school Karsavina studied with P. A. Gerdt, who had been for a long period the pride and essence of our ballet. For beauty of figure or gesture, for distinction of manner or stage expression, no other dancer could equal him. His dramatic powers were a real inspiration, besides being extraordinarily varied. His classical dancing was exceptional in its nobility, while his consummate art of mime produced everywhere the deepest impression.

No dancer could find a better partner in *pas de deux* or *adagio*. He took a loving interest in training Karsavina, whose talents so nearly resembled his own. In the graceful, delicate, and fascinating child with the pale face and strange eyes he quickly foresaw the coming artist, and set himself loyally to lay a solid foundation for her budding genius.

School training, however, is not everything. Let it be ever so conscientious and detailed, it can never give that wider and deeper outlook which comes later with years of experience. Actual appearance on the stage is the real source of that personal unfolding in the course of which the artist, herself eager to create, ceases to copy others. However gifted a child may prove at school, a pupil she remains. She may have intuition, charm, but as yet has no initiative, no artistic audacity. She hesitates and doubts, for her temperament is still growing. Her style displays no particular individuality—no real depth. For some time to come its general outline will carry the impress of school classicism.

THE truth of the matter is that a dancer's career is an exacting one which entails much responsibility. It demands strenuous daily practice, similar to that required of the pianist and violinist. It needs incessant study. Throughout her entire theatrical career the dancer must toil toward perfection.

For that reason there is attached to every important choreographic school a dancing class for *coryphées* who have completed their rudimentary training. Whatever talents a dancer may possess, she will achieve nothing without constant attention to technique. Therefore, the classical dancing school is the foundation of the ballet, and leads to whatever is valuable in the way of technical accomplishment. The school is indispensable to what is known as the ancient classical ballet, with its innumerable *variations*, *pas de deux*, and *adagios* ; its *pointes*, its *pirouettes* ; its various figures ; its difficult and purely mechanical business. And it is equally essential to the so-called new ballet, which, while discarding the mechanical part of choreography, unites dancing and music in one indivisible whole. In a way, the new ballet has simplified the external form while developing the inner sense of dancing; it has achieved plastic and rhythmic value. In all good art there is a seeming simplicity which requires for its perfection an infinity of technical knowledge and experience.

To continue—the classical school of dancing resembles the study of counterpoint and harmony in musical composition. A composer who is efficient in these sciences is potential master of both the old and the modern styles, while one unacquainted with the true essentials of technique is incapable of composing anything. It is the same for the dancer. Such truths are elementary. If they need constant repetition, it is because even accomplished performers will express the curious and mistaken view that no training is required for the new ballet.

At St. Petersburg, old Johannsen's class was just such an academy of ancient classical dancing, a school of choregraphic counterpoint. His principles and methods were strictly classic. They were the development of technical details; insistence on the strictest correctitude in the positions of the head, arms, feet, and body; the preservation of strength and precision. From these rules he allowed no deviation whatsoever.

Perhaps his training was soulless and dry, but, nevertheless, it was indispensable. It was not intended that the dancers should remain for ever tied to such classic principles, or that they should perpetually demonstrate them on the stage; what was meant was that the academies should provide a secure foundation for later unrestrained individual production of talent.

Karsavina passed through this academy during the first year of her independent existence as a dancer. And, as we have seen, it was in the study of this dry technical side of her art that she encountered her greatest difficulties. Again, it was these same details of virtuosity, technique, and precision that for a long time she failed to master. Indeed, it is only during the last five years that, without impairing the individualism of her talents, she has become, from the standpoint of technique, a first-class artist—I may say, an exceptional dancer of genius. She had to struggle patiently and stubbornly in this direction. She had gone to Signora Beretta for this purpose; the Italian school being specially famed for the due development of technique.

For this reason, also, she studied under E. Cecchetti, celebrated at St. Petersburg as a teacher of classical dancing, whose methods

strengthened her physique, insured her powers of resistance, and perfected the precision of her plastic interpretations.

Cecchetti was himself a famous dancer of the Italian school of virtuosity. Having made himself adept, also, in the spirit of the Russian ballet, he set aside in his teaching all the exaggerations of the Italian classical tradition, using them in his class merely as exercises, as a kind of dancing gymnastics. He did not believe in reproducing them on the stage, for he did not consider them of artistic value. For a long time Karsavina studied under him, and certainly is indebted to him for much of her present technical force. It is also due to him that, while her technique is now perfect, she has lost none of her individuality, and preserves in her dancing all the fragrance and loveliness of lyrical poetry.

Another teacher who played an important part in her technical training was E. P. Sokolova, ex-dancer of the Imperial Theatres.

'I attended Madame Sokolova's class for three years,' Karsavina writes in her *Recollections*. 'Her advice was exceedingly valuable to me. For it was with her that I studied the long ballets of Petipa and St. Leon. She herself had danced them when *première danseuse* at the *Mariynsky (Imperial Ballet) Theatre*. Those who had seen her on the stage considered her to be wonderfully graceful and to possess a remarkable talent in the art of mime. She was very conscientious in her teaching, and after she had left the stage, devoted herself entirely to her pupils.

'If, for some reason or other, she was unable to attend my rehearsal of a new *rôle*, she would ring me up on the telephone and —humming the melody of my *variations* or *adagio*—would question me, up to the smallest details, regarding my execution of the various steps.'

These were Karsavina's principal teachers. They worked with her, developing and perfecting those great attributes which at the outset of her career seemed in a measure to have remained concealed.

LET us return to Karsavina's appearances on the St. Petersburg stage. At that time the Imperial Theatre boasted of a constellation of great dancers whose like had never been seen on any other stage in the world.

The greatest of these, Anna Pavlova, had become already the glorious artist whom all Russia and all Europe admire. She was so light of foot, so seemingly severed from the earth, as to appear part of the air itself. A reincarnation of Taglioni had appeared, but of greater technical skill. Remarkable as a creator of new forms, Pavlova excelled in the arts both of pantomime and drama.

M. F. Kshesinskaïa was a dancer of extraordinary technique. For her, Italian virtuosity had no secrets. In the matter of precise technique nothing troubled her—neither *fouettés*, *entrechats*, complicated *pirouettes*, nor those other intricate details of technique characteristic of the Italian school of the nineteenth century. Again, she pleased every one by her representations of the dramatic portions of Petipa's old *répertoire*, such, for example, as *Esmeralda* and the opera of *Fenella*.

V. T. Trefilova was another star of great magnitude in classical technique. Her dancing had strength and precision, rhythm and virtuosity, as well as the loveliness and grace of youth. Her movements were softer than those of Kshesinskaïa. They had nothing abrupt or angular about them, as was sometimes the case with the latter. Her manner was more elegant, and was much appreciated.

O. O. Preobrajenskaïa was the personification of mischievous coquetry, graceful, but given a little, perhaps, to preciosity of style. She was possessed, also, of remarkable technical skill, developed to the minutest detail and with much taste. She knew that certain limits were not to be exceeded, and never permitted herself to transgress them in order to secure a cheap success. Some of her dances had a touch of artistic exaggeration and humour, but though gay, she was always discreet. Her creation, for example, of ' the little sailor ' has been adopted generally by the theatre. She was, besides, an excellent pantomimist in choregraphic comedy. . . . *Javotte*, *Svanilda* in *Coppélia* ; *Lise* in *La Fille Mal Gardée*. Finally, there were her exceptional musical capabilities, with their measured sense of rhythm and their gift for rendering a melody plastic in movement and dumb show.

I have purposely mentioned briefly the principal gifts of these 'stars' in order to show that, not only were the greatest living exponents of choregraphy there assembled, but, also, that the performers were of exceptional artistic power.

Into this charmed circle, timidly and somewhat unsteadily, stepped the youthful Karsavina; uncertain, perhaps unaware of her powers. There appeared to be nothing left for her to do. Everything had been successfully—and *how* successfully—accomplished by others. Still, she was an artist with the artist's soul. The spirit of drama was in her, already unconsciously striving to create. As with every true craftsman, who hesitates before the immensity of his task and desires, at least, to give it the impress of his own individuality, doubt weighed heavily on Karsavina's heart, retarding her first steps, impeding her first efforts.

We have seen that in her *Recollections* she explained this period of failure by a temporary nervous breakdown following on severe illness. But I am inclined to place the causes elsewhere—deeper. I would seek for them in her very natural hesitation when confronted by an arduous task, in a want of confidence in her own powers, in a certain degree of bashfulness before that brilliant company of 'great authorities'; a bashfulness to which every true votary of art is liable when his talent is still on probation, not yet revealed, not matured. . . . Karsavina's genius was slowly gathering force, soon to burst forth with irresistible strength. . . .

I am all the more inclined to believe this because, for some time after her illness, even when quite recovered, she was still unable to show herself mistress of her dancing. For a long while her dancing continued to lack power and precision. It seemed to be seeking unsuccessfully for its own natural expression, for its final individual form. . . .

She conveyed the impression of possessing artistic faculties of a high order, but of not knowing how to make use of them. She would dance carelessly, almost negligently; she seemed to be employed in an ungracious task, grudging even the effort which mere necessity compelled her to make. There was neither inspiration nor temperament in her performances. She appeared to be taking no pains whatever. While a section of the public applauded her, despite her shortcomings, the rest remained mute, perhaps sorry for a dancer whose great natural gifts it was impossible to mistake.

I myself, I confess, religiously recorded her failures in my choregraphic notes. I do not know whether my criticism had at the time either harmful or beneficial results for the dancer, or whether its effects were merely futile . . . but I could not refrain from writing of what I saw. And now I know that at that period Karsavina was passing through the painful ordeal of a true artist who doubts his powers—or, at least, their degree. . . .

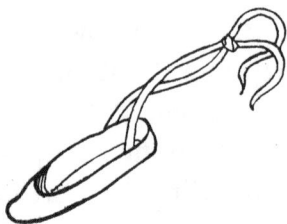

ON her road to fame Karsavina had every facility accorded to her by our ballet direction. She was never put in the background as so many were. She was immediately assigned good parts, and not restricted to unimportant *rôles*. She was never relegated to the chorus; while in the year following her *début* in 1903 she was already dancing in a one-act ballet—*Le Réveil de Flore* (music by R. Drigo)—in which she achieved conspicuous success. Notwithstanding the imperfections manifest in her dancing, she was praised both by public and critics. It was concerning this earliest independent part of hers that K. A. Skalkovsky wrote a very clever article. She had a splendid reception, being repeatedly called before the curtain and applauded to the echo. Nevertheless, I adhered to my own opinion that her success came largely and naturally out of the springtime of the dancer's youth, and was due to her radiant beauty, her exceptionally graceful figure, and to the appealing and fascinating expression of joy which radiated from every detail of her presence.

SEARCHINGS

AT the period of which I write it was not the custom for our ballet to go abroad. Italian dancers had not yet disappeared from the European stage. Every theatre of importance considered it essential to include at least one in the cast. Our own stage has seen all of them, without exception, from the most insignificant to the most gifted—such as Virginia Zucchi and Pierrina Legnani. The system of favouring without distinction everything foreign and of depreciating everything Russian had, of course, resulted in the Italian stars, big and little, obscuring native talent and preventing our dancers from receiving their due. On the other hand, the Italians were useful both to our dancers and to our choregraphic stage. V. Zucchi demonstrated the value and importance of pantomime. After her time, it was no longer possible to be contented with the scanty and conventional mimetic effects of the primitive ballet. It was no longer sufficient merely to appear. It was necessary to act, to produce drama—that is to say, not merely conventional gesture but dramatic expression, emphasised by the dancer's whole being.

After P. Legnani, no one could dance 'anyhow,' by merely following the music more or less, or expect to satisfy with the earlier forms of technique. Our dancers set themselves bravely to the task of mastering mechanical difficulties, and soon a cast could be got together without calling upon the Italians. Dancers like A. Pavlova and M. Kshesinskaïa displayed remarkable gifts in the art of mime; while the other classic exponents I have recorded became celebrated for their technical skill. Not only were our performers no longer inferior to the Italians, but they excelled them. While retaining all the precision of Italian technique, they softened its angularity and exaggerations, and gave it a grace and roundness of movement lacked by the Southern school.

Thus terminated the Italian invasion, developed to excess under the management of T. A. Vsevolojsky. The director of the Imperial Theatres who succeeded him, V. A. Teliakovsky, limited his choice, as far as possible, to native artists and excluded the foreign element. Strange to say, this particular director was never fully credited with a decision so beneficial to our ballet. Though he gave our dancers confidence in themselves, Teliakovsky was for long fiercely upbraided by the critics, who unanimously condemned him for every kind of mistake of which they considered him guilty in the important and responsible *rôle* entrusted to him.

At the *Grand Opera*, where the admission of foreign performers was carefully avoided, Kshesinskaïa, with Nijinsky as partner, appeared in Delibes' *Sylvie*. At the same time Anna Pavlova received offers of engagements abroad, both for herself and for a troupe of eight or ten performers who should accompany her. Preobrajenskaïa began dancing in Berlin; Karsavina at Prague.

Karsavina was one of the first Russian dancers to set the fashion of dancing abroad. It was in 1908 that she obtained the Prague engagement. There is in Prague a Czech (not German) theatre called the *Narodny Divaldo*. It is a large building, beautiful architecturally, and decorated in charming taste. Here the young dancer appeared with her yet unripe talents. Prague was greatly interested in the ballet, and had possessed for some time a school of its own, where the Terpsichorean art was taken seriously, not regarded as merely transitory and accessory, but as having firmly established roots and traditions. At the time of Karsavina's visit the public of Prague had for favourite a little girl of eleven, named Stepanko. Beyond all doubt she was gifted and gave great hopes of future success. Unfortunately, like the general run of child prodigies, she did not realise them. Many years have passed, and her name remains unknown to the programmes and publicity of the European stage.

The conductor of the theatre was a well-known Czech composer, Nedbal, author of the ballet *Grandmother's Tales*, of which the

subjects were taken from the *Sleeping Beauty*, the *Frog Princess*, and the *Goblin Ass*. Nedbal's custom was to unite several fairy tales in one, and he did this for Karsavina. Taking Tchaikovsky's *Casse Noisette* as a foundation, he added several episodes out of *La Belle au Bois Dormant*, by the same composer. Notwithstanding the mixture, the ballet interested. The themes and music were combined by an artist; and the ballet, which was long, contained six important *tableaux*. It was produced by the *maître-de-ballet* of the theatre, an Italian named Viscussi, who was, at the same time, chief dancer. As Karsavina's partner, he assisted her loyally, though apt to fail her at difficult moments.

The ballet opened with the prologue of *La Belle au Bois Dormant*, where the wicked fairy *Carabosse* changes the newborn boy into a pair of nutcrackers, and the good fairy promises to restore him later to his human shape. Then followed scenes of the 'fir-tree,' of the 'mice-war with wooden soldiers,'[1] 'snowflakes,' 'the kingdom of sweets,' and an apotheosis. The production was good, but the dancers of the *Prague Theatre* left much to be desired. One danced well—the one I have mentioned—but the rest were indifferent. Even the *pointe* seemed unknown to them.

Karsavina appeared during the Prague Exhibition. She was received with true Slav cordiality, for both public and theatrical direction greeted her with enthusiasm. She was acclaimed as a gifted artist from a great nation, a visitor as well as a charming personality. Her youth and beauty, the freshness of her promising, if as yet undeveloped, talent, appealed generally to every one. Her title was never other than 'our dear guest and the famous *diva*.' With a ballet theme taken from Hoffmann, a continuous interest of movement, music by Tchaikovsky, a favourite of the Czechs, and, lastly, the beautiful dancer, already revealing future genius, everything tended to an exceptional success, which, in fact, was achieved. . . . A house crowded at every performance with a bright and cheerful audience accorded the dancer one long ovation.

After the first rehearsal, the direction offered her a part in seven performances instead of four, as originally arranged. In addition to that, she was offered engagements at Vienna and Buda Pesth during Lent and the spring, engagements which she was unable to accept owing to her contracts with the Crown stage. She

[1] Stories from Hoffmann's *Serapion Brethren*.

nevertheless undertook to return the following year, and this promise she kept.

On her second visit to Prague she appeared with still greater success, at the same theatre as before, in the ballets *Giselle* and *Une Nuit d'Egypte*.[1] She was greeted as an old friend and favourite. She no longer felt shy as on her first appearance abroad in responsible *rôles* and before an unfamiliar public. Karsavina has preserved the kindest feelings for the good people of Prague, whose warm welcome consoled her for the growing coolness of her friends at St. Petersburg. She appeared brighter at Prague, as if she felt the return of inspiration, a renewed confidence in herself and in her future success. Nevertheless, on her return to Russia, she was assailed again by depression, by the *malaise* so painfully reflected in her dancing.

MEANWHILE, prior to her visits to Prague, she had been given new parts in small ballets at the Crown theatres. We may, therefore, again refer with advantage to her early career on the stage. In 1904 she took the leading part in Glazounoff's graceful ballet, *Ruses d'Amour*,[2] and another in the older ballet *Graziella*. A cold critic of the day, who signed himself Z., and who accorded praise very sparingly, particularly to beginners, was delighted with Karsavina's impersonation of the 'Countess' in Glazounoff's ballet. He gives a very accurate *résumé* of the young dancer's abilities in his notes :—' The small, but individualistic, ballet, *Ruses d'Amour*, afforded Madame Karsavina an opportunity for revealing all the splendour of her brilliant attainments. She is not only a remarkable dancer, but a true " artist," endowed with powers of evoking the period of action as well as of affording it mimetic expression. Madame Karsavina was the " Countess," not only of the text of the programme, but also of real life. This was especially noteworthy when one remembers

[1] Afterwards called *Cléopâtre*.
[2] Also called *The Trial of Damis* and *La Demoiselle Paysanne*.

other countesses and marchionesses, who overwhelm the stage. Her unstudied elegance, free of preciosity, fascinated the audience and evoked their loud applause. Madame Karsavina is, without a doubt, a rising star of the first magnitude in ballet.'

Karsavina continued to appear in other ballets, in solos. In 1905 she took the part of the Spaniard in *The Fairy of the Dolls*. This was a German affair, 'Russianised' by St. Petersburg *maîtres-de-ballet*—the brothers Legat. It contained a number of insipid banalities, German waltzes and other musical numbers, collected at random, without consideration either for homogeneity or musical style. It was a medley of Russian and German methods, a senseless musical *pot-pourri*, similar to that which foreign conductors are everywhere so fond of putting before music-hall audiences. An insignificant conception such as that of the Spanish doll was obviously unlikely to inspire Karsavina, who already had been accorded opportunities for dancing in parts conceived on a far grander scale. Moreover, she was scarcely suited to the interpretation of the ballet-master's idea of the Spanish doll, with its interminable mechanical movements that were only monotonous. She danced unwillingly, hesitatingly, without conviction or precision. Her attitudes were incorrect and careless. However, she was beginning to find favour again with the public, and success attended her even in a part like this.

On the same night Pavlova appeared in the famous *grand pas* in *Paquita*, where a success, due to the wonderful effect she gave of flying and the general brilliancy of her performance, overshadowed Karsavina's accomplishments as the doll. I mention this in order to insist again on the enormous difficulties Karsavina was called upon to surmount through being perpetually in rivalry with a surrounding galaxy of talent which had already achieved fame. This circumstance must be borne in mind.

A few years have elapsed since we learned to know the Spaniard *Kitri* in the ballet *Don Quichotte* . . . one of Karsavina's most remarkable creations, both in colour and style. We need not be surprised if she disdained to look for the outline and colour of ethnographic choregraphy in the primitive image of the Spanish doll. *Don Quichotte*, full of *finesse* and complex beauty, which Karsavina grasped so ably and felt so delicately, was as far apart from the crude jerkiness of the child's plaything as the poles are from one another. To achieve such a transition many seasons of study and practice had been required.

After this *danse de caractère* and the unbecoming *rôle* of the Spanish doll, Karsavina was allotted a purely classical theme, a *variation* to the tableau *Visions* of Glazounoff's *Raymonda*. In this branch of her art she had not yet found her true self. While Marie Petipa was dancing with extraordinary beauty the brilliant part of *Panadéros*, Karsavina's dancing passed almost unnoticed. It was through such experiences as these that the young artist had to pass nightly—yet in *Paquita*, in the famous classical *pas de trois* which she undertook with A. Vaganova and N. G. Legat, Karsavina appeared to be suddenly endowed with new life. She overcame her misgivings, and danced with such perfection that, in response to continuous applause, the *pas* was repeated for her benefit.

CONTROL over herself once achieved, Karsavina danced better at her every appearance. She often performed insignificant parts and *variations* in ballets where O. Preobrajenskaïa, A. Pavlova, and others took leading *rôles*. The public and the critics naturally devoted their attention first to such brilliant dancers, but these no longer obscured Karsavina. She was now regarded with interest, and within a brief period there was assigned to her a number of small parts of no real importance, but which gave her the stage experience she required and accustomed her not to be shy. Though unimportant, they needed continual practice. In this way she danced a small *variation* out of *The Stream*, a minor part in *Don Quichotte*, the fisher-girl in *La Fille du Pharaon*; enjoying no less success in these trifles than did Trefilova, who usually took them. She also replaced Trefilova in *La Bayadère*. In this she greatly pleased the public with her pretty, slightly affected grace and the elegance of her *pointes*. Many people came to the conclusion that, not only was she not inferior to Trefilova, but was superior to her. She was equally at home in the *Animated Statues* of the ballet *Koniok Gorbounok* (*Le Petit Cheval Bossu*), in which her classical dancing began to take precise shape and correct and definite outline in a purely classical manner.

She still had to display her powers in character dances, as, for example, in the 'little Russians' in the same ballet. In this composition, of a purely national ethnographical character, she was less successful, although it must be confessed that there are not many *strictly* ethnographical traits in this ballet. On December 12th, 1906, the benefit night for the *corps de ballet*, Karsavina was again called upon to dance a Spanish character dance, *Mazeppa* in *The Travelling Dancer*. And how great the progress made in the short period since the Spanish doll ! . . . She achieved a triumphant success, although Preobrajenskaïa was also interpreting Spanish dances. It should, however, be admitted that Spanish dancing was not altogether Preobrajenskaïa's style. In *Mazeppa* Karsavina suddenly disclosed an *élan* in which a keen observer might have detected for the first time that remarkable elegance which later became the chief characteristic of her dancing. This one of all her qualities was particularly noticeable in *Mazeppa*; also in the *pas classique hongrois* in *Raymonda*, of which the last act was on the same programme.

THE end of 1906 held a place of importance in Karsavina's career. On December 17th the sixty-third performance—since its revival—of *Le Petit Cheval Bossu* took place—with the original *mise-en-scène*. The ballet was well known and the public tired of it; yet particular interest was attached to the performance, because in it young Karsavina made her *début* as leading dancer. She had danced in small one-act ballets, such as *Ruses d'Amour* and *Le Réveil de Flore*, *rôles* less responsible than the one she took in the old classical ballet in which the public had watched Legnani, Kshesinskaïa, Geltzer, and others. Still, in the words of the fable—' A wild flower was attached to a bunch of carnations and became fragrant.' To speak without allegory, it must be recognised that Karsavina achieved on this occasion not a superficial success, but a genuine one, in a difficult part for a young dancer. She was quite excellent at times, accomplishing various brilliant steps (*ballonés*) in the *Nereids*, as well as *pointes* in *variations*. Her graceful *attitudes* and *port de bras* were particularly admired, the mazurka and *finale* in the third act being especially successful. Karsavina danced the Russian dance in plastic and rounded fashion, which, with her expressive pantomime, presented a real *tableau de genre* in soft and exquisite colouring.

Naturally, defects were noticeable in the performance. Karsavina's dancing still lacked self-possession and decision. She hesitated between moments of timidity and moments of growing daring. Her performance was uneven, like a mosaic; every step seemingly executed independently and with a lack of homogeneity very prejudicial to the impression as a whole. The imperfections were, of course, due to a *début* in a responsible character which already had been interpreted by so many distinguished performers. She was hampered by these traditions and by the laws which they had laid down for the execution of the part. Very few would have dared to break through such a habit or to shake such a foundation.

Defects were noticeable, also, in her interpretation of the *Girl King*.[1] Karsavina scarcely evoked the image of the queenly 'daughter of the moon and sister of the sun.' . . . Rather, she was the little bird of the Russian tale.

What was the conclusion to be drawn? I think that it was too soon for Karsavina to have undertaken such heavy work as *Le Petit Cheval Bossu*. Although undoubtedly gifted, she was as yet very young; she had much to learn, especially in the matter of the individuality of her dancing. One would have liked to see this wild flower developing more independently—under good guidance, of course—and not relying for her fragrance so much on the carnations. Her dancing had to be her own, and not an imitation of others. A mediocre original is worth in art more than the best copy. All these reflections arose at what may be styled her examination in her first leading character. Yet, when all is said and due account taken and allowances made for the nervousness of a *début*, nothing really cancelled the pleasant

[1] Tsar Vierge

Thamar Karsavina in Petrouchka, from the statue by Soudbinin

impression made by Karsavina in the great *rôle* of *Le Petit Cheval Bossu*.

This successful appearance of a new leading dancer showed the public and critics what remarkable choregraphic abilities the Crown stage held in reserve in the person of Karsavina, a child who had started comparatively young and who had borne with credit so highly responsible a *rôle*. Yet, after a triumph like this, the young dancer was put back to easier and insignificant parts.

The following year, 1907, was unimportant in the evolution of Karsavina's talents. She could be neither interested nor inspired to create serious and complex work and pantomime when obliged to dance such trifles as the *Little White Cat* in *La Belle au Bois Dormant!* . . . She did not seem to discover even the correct tone for this small ' *tableau de genre*,' although as the *Fairy of the Lilacs* in the same ballet she was very fascinating. It was her first appearance in this exceedingly insignificant affair; nevertheless, in the course of its one *variation*, so brilliantly did she execute a series of *entrechats* that she evoked the overwhelming applause of an enchanted audience.

She then danced with L. Kyasht in *variations* and dances of the ballet *Kalkabrino*. Again she was successful, though giving the impression that such trifles as these no longer inspired one who felt within her the growth of high creative power. Now follow her performances with Nijinsky.

Karsavina's first effort with Nijinsky was a *pas de deux* from the ballet *Roxane*. It was a triumph of classical dancing. At that time neither of the pair had reached the summit of their artistic development, though their talents were never in question. Both were young, graceful, and possessed of attractive physique. In delightful costumes, they made a picture not often witnessed even on such a stage as was that of the *Mariynsky Theatre*.

I say ' was ' advisedly, because I am writing these lines in the first year of the Revolution, and can predict nothing as to what attitude the future State government may take towards the ex-Imperial Theatres. Still, I do not believe that an art which has reached so high a state of perfection as our ballet can possibly cease to exist. Even should the State subsidies hitherto granted be withdrawn, people of means will be there to prevent the art from perishing in Russia.

To continue the story of Karsavina and Nijinsky. They danced together often, both on the Crown stage and abroad. But I will speak of that in its proper place. Now, I propose to give Karsavina's own opinion of a wholly exceptional dancer as it is found in her *Recollections*.

'The history of Nijinsky's progress on the stage differs from that of our other dancers. At our schools great attention is generally paid to the special improvement of gifted scholars; yet as a little boy Nijinsky was neglected. His brilliant abilities were revealed unexpectedly, almost by accident. They burst on public and critics as a revelation, as a surprise. Prior to his *début* he was assigned a small part in *Le Réveil de Flore*, that of *Aquilon*. He had to make two small entries and, in a few leaps, to cross the stage. At his first bound a murmur of wonder came from the spectators!...

'It was some time after this before he made his first great success. When he was rehearsing it was customary for other artists to come to the practice room during a lesson and ask him to show them his great step (*ballon*). The modest and obliging boy would go to the middle of the room and perform a few wonderful *entrechats*. After his public appearance, we often danced together *pas de deux*, which had been specially introduced for us into the ballets of our *répertoire*.'

A year or so after Karsavina's appearance as leading dancer in *Le Petit Cheval Bossu* she was allocated a part in Tchaikovsky's *Lac des Cygnes*, perhaps one of the most difficult ballets in our *répertoire*. The *Girl King* in *Le Petit Cheval Bossu* is a purely dancing *rôle* which offers no particular difficulties to a good dancer; and the ballet, like a great many old-time ballets, is a mere *divertissement*, with no particular choreographic idea or dramatic form. On the other hand, the part of *Odetta-Odilia* contains a succession of the most difficult steps, besides considerable opportunities for pantomime; and, moreover, the *Lac des Cygnes* is an integral creation of remarkable power, full of the romanticism of a romantic century. It had been P. Legnani's masterpiece. She had introduced into it her famous thirty-two *fouettés*, a feat which gave no peace to those of our dancers who prided themselves on their technique. Every one was compelled to strive to accomplish, at any cost, this inartistic feat of classical dancing. A few achieved it—Kshesinskaïa, Trefilova, and Sedova. But Karsavina's artistic sense rebelled against the *fouettés* in the second act. Besides, she was too young and inexperienced in technical virtuosity to attempt such a task. The *coda* had to be altered and made easier for her, a change which occasioned profound chagrin and disappointment to many adherents of strict ballet law.

Karsavina continued to appear in her famous part in *Le Lac des Cygnes*, and it is strange now to remember her earlier searchings after herself, the first tentative trial efforts of her young genius! In *Le Lac des Cygnes* she has attained to such perfection of beauty and expression, both in dance and romantic pantomime, that it is hard to imagine anything greater in plastic realisation. Nevertheless, to my mind, her *début* in the part was a doubtful success. Her dancing still lacked self-confidence, and there was an absence of homogeneity in her creation of the character. However, there were plastic poses and dramatic moments of immense value. They augured well for the future. But as a whole, owing to the absence of cohesion, a definite picture was wanting. Her flashes of brilliancy suggested rather the gifted artist seeking the glimmering light of an only half-realised ideal, or a creative imagination unable as yet, owing to youth and inexperience, to take determinate shape.

The transition from the pseudo-popular *Girl King* to the romantic *Odetta* was abrupt. It was no less so from the romanticism of *Odetta* to the antique style of *Actea* in *Eunice*.

Eunice was produced for the first time on February 17th, 1908. It was Fokine's first essay in the new form of ballet. In reality it was a link between the old style and the new, between the art known to Petipa, the last *maître-de-ballet*, and the daring innovations of Fokine.

Pavlova, taking in her own beautiful way the leading part in the new ballet, gave it fascinating popularity with a public which delighted in anything new—by a beauty that shocked neither their ancient beliefs nor traditions. For in *Eunice* Fokine had not as yet travelled very far afield from the old laws. He, too, was seeking for himself. The part of *Actea* is not a very big one, but Karsavina, enamoured of the sword dance, gave it the vogue it acquired.

As a matter of fact, *Eunice* was an answer to a question

interesting every one at that time :—Was there a future for the school of Isadora Duncan ? That is to say, was its further evolution to be expected ? Was it adaptable to a big stage, and to what degree ? Or was it to be limited—as to dancing—to the concert-room ? Fokine answered these questions by his essay to adapt the Duncan school to a large theatre and to a two-act ballet. He was the first to introduce on our stage the bare feet, the plastic movements and attitudes, the ancient *chitons*, the spirit of the new school. Isadora Duncan was present herself at the performance. From that moment a manner disdained and misunderstood by former *maîtres-de-ballet* took its lawful place in choreographic production. Following *Eunice*, and in the same year, Fokine presented *Une Nuit d'Egypte* at a private performance ; also the first sketch of his celebrated *Chopiniana*, which travelled round the world under the title of *Les Sylphides*, but which at its first inception bore the awkward name *Ballet for Chopin's Music*. The whole style of the ballet; the long skirts, the simply parted, fillet-circled hair; Chopin's dreamy, romantic music; and the simple classical dancing in the manner of Taglioni; all gave an unexpected illusion of novelty combined with a true artistic sense. The success achieved strengthened the newborn fame of the *maître-de-ballet*.

Karsavina, who danced a waltz of soft, ethereal, lyrical cadence, was the embodiment of an old-time romantic lithograph. She was drawing nearer the end of her probation and of her self-searchings. After this performance, no doubt remained as to the nature of the dance which best satisfied Karsavina's spirit. It was the lyrical dance . . . the fanciful dream, the song of poetic, rhythmic melody. It was in Hartmann's ballet of *The Red Flower*, in the lovely music of the *Rose*, that she found once more the expression that gave her dancing its chief beauty.

In the same year she was allotted a *rôle* in another big ballet—*Le Corsaire*. She did it complete justice. The type of *Medora*, the romantic Greek girl of Byron's poem, exactly suited the young *ballerina*, who in the image presented was able to combine physical beauty, dramatic acting, and choreographic intelligence. In the miming of the second act she gave proof, not only of great delicacy of expression, but also of a vigour never overstepping the bounds of refinement. Her rendering of Birbanto's crime was full of strength and subtlety. In the *adagio* (*pas de deux*, second act), she was graceful and tender; in the *variations*, vivacious and brilliant. In that of *Le Jardin Animé*, as in *Le Corsaire*, her success was manifest, her reception whole-hearted and deserved. I, at all events, no longer recognised the previously *nonchalant* Karsavina in the dancer whose performance displayed so much splendour and colour. She completed a fortunate year (1908) with the visit to Prague, to which I have referred already.

In truth, it had been for her a period of self-searching—a period when the genius awake in her soul strove to break through—when she heard the imperative call, hitherto sounding only faintly in her consciousness. From the gay and mischievous *Little White Cat* she throws herself into the drama of *Odetta-Odilia*. Now she is seeking herself in a character dance; now in a classical *variation*; now, again, in a commonplace *pas de deux*. She is searching in the ancient *Actea*, in the lyric *Rose*, in Byron's *Medora*, or else in the dreamer Chopin. . . . She knows not when or whence the final summons of her art will come. Something is still wanting, and, tortured by an unsatisfied desire, she indefatigably seeks her sphere. . . . Disillusioned at one moment, a successful essay revives her. She goes through all the agonies of creation, and still cannot determine what she is. But, whatever she is doing, successfully or not, she is gaining advantage, because, while seeking, she tries her strength and acquires self-knowledge.

Karsavina's years of self-searchings were over. She had emerged definitely on the radiantly illumined path of Fame. . . .

THE PATH OF FAME

SUDDENLY, almost unconsciously, after many severe tests and trials, Karsavina had reached the cross roads whence *her* road led to celebrity. She had become a true artist, one who not only worked conscientiously in strict accordance with the technicalities of her art, but who had also acquired a real comprehension of it. And only the artist who thoroughly masters all the technical peculiarities and material forms of her art ever reaches perfect freedom of creative power.

' *La forme n'est rien, mais rien n'est sans la forme.*'

However lofty and inspired a composer's originating fantasy may be, if he is ignorant of the theory of music or incompetent to master its multiple details, his dream remains in the spirit. It may be platonic, but it does not materialise. On the other hand, the artist who has freed himself of the obstacles of technical reproduction in the plastic forms of art is able to give his genius play and consciously to follow his imagination wherever it may lead him. The spirit of art can be conquered only after a victory has been gained over the material side. . . .

At the point now reached, Karsavina had grown into an artist of more or less definite views regarding the various schools, styles and periods of choregraphy. With study and knowledge she undertook several revivals of M. Petipa's old *répertoire*. She witnessed the beginning of ballet reform. She saw the effort to free it from routine, hide-bound laws and customs, from the mmobility of its academic postures; in short, from everything which prohibited the slightest deviation from secular tradition. It was with her help that Fokine had begun his revolutionary experiments. Fokine destroyed nothing. He observed that the old well-trodden road ended in a *cul de sac*. His original genius could not be satisfied with merely marking time. He did not care to create new grooves scarcely differing from the old ones; he did not care to plan a fresh road by the side of the old and well-worn highway. . . .

Karsavina, a clever woman, with a delicate understanding of her art, had formed very clear and definite opinions of the two roads. She has given a brief summary of them in her *Recollections*, and her profession of faith is interesting. She describes the old and new ballets as follows:—

'At the outset of my career, Marius Petipa was coming to the end of his profession as *maître-de-ballet*.[1] He had had long experience and had done much useful service to choregraphy. He had a remarkable command of mass on the stage, and sometimes the forms taken by his *ballabilles*[2] showed considerable imagination. But his productions were all founded on the same formula. An inevitable "*divertissement*" brought his ballets to an ever happy conclusion; while such of his heroes for whom anything but a tragic end was an historical impossibility found themselves crowned in a final apotheosis. His ballets tended to be "*féeries*." In his later years he made some attempts to modernise his art to accord more nearly with the present time, but he never felt at ease when making these efforts, and they were unsuccessful. His ballets, which even now have not disappeared from the *répertoire* of the *Mariynsky Theatre*, were crowded with marches and processions which often interrupted, without any kind of logical excuse, long continuous scenes of pantomime and beautifully composed classical dances.'

This was Karsavina's view of Petipa's productions. And those who were acquainted with the old master's interminable ballets, which comprised for so many years the whole *répertoire* of our choregraphic stage, will agree with an opinion so carefully and delicately expressed.

While criticising the old *maître-de-ballet* she also gives her opinion of Fokine, the creator of the new ballet.

[1] For an account of Petipa's career, see Svetlov (V.), *Le Ballet Contemporain*, Brunoff, Paris, 1912, pp. 5—18.

[2] The word *ballabille* signifies a dance executed by a large number of persons, such as the general *corps-de-ballet*. The word was introduced into France and other countries by Carlo Blasis. (*Vide* Blasis, *History of Dancing*.)

'It is only just to say a few words about Michel Fokine. He was the first to realise that the actual forms of the ballet were old-fashioned and worn out. He was also the first to awaken the art of dancing from its lethargy. The majority of the public took a view hostile to his innovations. He was looked upon as a revolutionary, and was supported only by a loyal few who gathered round him. He produced Anton Rubinstein's ballet, *The Vine*, at a charity performance. It had been written for some special occasion, but not performed, owing to difficulties and unsuitabilities in the music. Yet as produced by Fokine it proved a brilliant success. Anna Pavlova, Michel Fokine and myself danced the leading parts. It was never repeated, but I attach the greatest importance to its production. It was Fokine's *début* as *maître-de-ballet*, and the starting-point of a new orientation in scenic choreography. Each successive production by Fokine won him more sympathy and recognition. Since then—I am speaking of St. Petersburg—he has given *Eunice*, *Une Nuit d'Egypte*, *Le Carnaval*, *Le Pavillon d'Armide*, *Chopiniana* (*Les Sylphides*), *Islamei*, and *Papillons*. His reputation as an exceptional ballet director is now unquestioned, and he has fully deserved his success. Moreover, it is impossible to judge of the entire range of his art by what he has yet achieved. The greatest of his choreographic performances still await him.'

In such a restrained and almost careful manner (the *Recollections* date from 1912) the dancer's admiration is expressed for the new ballet and its creator. Her prophecy has been fulfilled. Since 1912, Fokine has created his masterpieces, the *Polovetz* dances, *Schéhérazade*, *Petrouchka*, *Le Spectre de la Rose*, *Narcisse*, and many others.

IT was in this mood of admiration for the new art that Karsavina went to Paris in 1909, at the invitation of S. P. Diaghileff.

'It was one of the most important stages in my career,' the dancer writes. 'On my first arrival in Paris, I must admit to feeling prejudiced against that city. I looked upon it as a scene of eternal pleasure, exceedingly frivolous and dangerous. Above all I was nervous of appearing provincial. My dismal forebodings were unfounded. Very pleasant surprises awaited me, and now there is no place that I like better than Paris. I can think of no other city where the public has greater delicacy of perception, a quicker comprehension and appreciation of artistic merit in the dance, and of artistic personality in the dancer. In the æsthetic atmosphere of the city, the latter develops with overwhelming rapidity.'

One passage more from the *Recollections* may be given concerning the Paris visit. The reader will find in it the dancer's artistic creed, beside a final outline of a personality whose views on art were well formed before she arrived there. It may, of course, be true that Karsavina's success in France was a little due to her holding this creed. In her the Parisians found something they understood, something with which they sympathised. It may account for the suddenness with which the enthusiasm both of critics and public kindled at almost the first sight of the dancer's talent, and for its remaining ever since at the same heat.

'It is always easier for me to speak of myself retrospectively. Looking back on the past years, I can see quite clearly both the people and the circumstances by which I have been influenced. I can see the elements that have helped in the evolution of my art, that have made me what I am. Still, it is not easy for me to state my *credo*. There are a few things about which I have formed a definite opinion, one that will not easily change. For instance, I am absolutely convinced that it is indispensable to possess great technical skill in art, in order to be able to interpret anything belonging to the marvellous and seemingly unreal. But this technique must be employed only for a purpose, and good taste must prevent one from exaggerating it, or from using it only as a means of showing off!

'The best technique is that which passes unnoticed and requires no apparent effort . . . a consummation not achieved by the gifted amateur! . . . Do I belong to the Italian or French school? I do not share the opinion of those who pretend that the first is superior to the second, neither am I of the opposite opinion. I love the *arabesque*, the beautiful lines of the French school, its disdain of useless acrobatics; but I appreciate as well the power of the Italian tradition. However, neither the one nor the other is of value without a true artistic individuality; without the help of the faint and often scarcely noticeable element of personality in art—and this is beyond analysis. It is just this infinitely delicate element which conceals from the onlooker the technicalities of the school. It raises dancing to the upper realms of art and poetry; to the empyrean, where burns the artist's soul.'

AFTER years of research, trial, experiment, hope, success and disappointment, the dancer had reached this lofty eminence of conception. The average spectator, who admires an artist on the stage, forgets that not only has she to overcome the physical effort of dancing, but also to unfold her artistic self. As Karsavina observes with much subtlety, this individuality is often unnoticed by, and incomprehensible to, the spectator. Yet it is that which gives the dance its fragrance, its indefinable charm, and its character. It is that indescribable something which, for lack of a better word, we call talent. And what is talent? No philosopher, no psychologist—no art critic even—has succeeded in defining it with even approximate precision. Where genius reigns, there is everything except mathematics! And if talent is the incessant and elemental manifestation of individuality in the material and technical forms of art, then Karsavina, on her arrival in Paris, was endowed indeed with a talent of a very remarkable kind. After long searchings she had succeeded in incorporating in the material elements of her dancing the varying harmonies of line, pose and movement; the complex design and architecture of choregraphic form; the divine spark of her personality. . . .

Later, we shall see the measure in which her spiritual nature blended with her material self and lifted it to a high level of plastic art. But first let us devote our attention to her early appearances in Paris.

Karsavina's reception at the *Théâtre du Châtelet* was magnificent, particularly when one remembers that in Paris she was unknown. Only a few people, specially interested in ballet matters (few at that period), had heard of her.

Her appearance in *L'Oiseau d'Or*—not to be confused with Stravinsky's *L'Oiseau de Feu*, which appeared much later—brought forth a storm of applause from the select Parisian audience which was present at the opening performance of Diaghileff's first season. It was a *pas de deux* from Tchaikovsky's *La Belle au Bois Dormant*. The name had been changed to emphasise the distinction between the old conception of the dance and the new one, which was extraordinary in fantasy, fairy-like in style, and, being decorated by Bakst, beautiful in colour.

Till now the Parisian public had been indifferent to classical theatrical dancing. French *ballerinas* were merely accustomed to perform the various mechanical steps considered the ordinary complement of operatic entertainment. The appearance of Karsavina with a partner having the power of Nijinsky had the effect of a revelation. It produced both wonder and ecstasy. I do not think that such applause was ever heard in any other theatre in the world. It even compelled the orchestra to stop playing.

And from that day Karsavina was the idol of Paris. . . .

Thus is tradition overthrown. . . .

Daily papers that had been in the habit of devoting to the French ballet a banal review of ten lines, with a sprinkling of commonplace compliments to the *ballerina* (no matter how she danced), appeared with articles a column long ! Portraits, snapshots, interviews, short biographies of the dancer appeared everywhere. Painters began to make drawings of the new star. Illustrated magazines were filled with her pictures. Karsavina pleased in every aspect—her physical appearance, her art, her costumes, her dancing. . . .

Robert Brusselle, himself an enthusiastically admiring critic, said in the *Figaro* that she had caused a ' deep sensation ' in Paris. He saw in her all the charms of classicism, and applied to her Despreaux' well-known formula :—' Grace of form—grace of attitude—grace of movement.' She had no rivals in her manner of dancing ; an opinion which other critics shared. ' She is faultless in all tangible themes proper to this earth—as she is in more ethereal conceptions—in her *port de bras*—in her tender grace and beauty of line. 'Her technique is refined, precise, assured, and strangely fascinating.'

Such were R. Brusselle's opinions about her. The praise accorded her by the entire French Press would fill several volumes. Not only the daily papers, but also the periodicals, gave long accounts of the performance. I will reproduce one other passage from the same critic, in which he gives a very correct appreciation of Karsavina's talents.

'She possesses much virtuosity, but never attempts to capture our surprise by a daring technique which would degrade dancing to the level of acrobatics. Her ideals are purer. She attracts and fascinates by the delicacy and tenderness of her movements, the grace of her attitudes, the appealing expression of her gestures. Hers are the visions of a far-off mythical region; she is the young and lovely daughter of classical choreography, who has proved possible a union between tradition and progress.'

It would be difficult to describe better or with more accuracy the substance of Karsavina's talent at the moment of its sudden and unexpected revelation in Paris. But I will no longer dwell on French criticism. I have quoted a few passages from it to show the deep sensation caused by Karsavina's appearance on the stage of the world's art-capital, and the success which followed. She had come to Paris young, lacking self-confidence, and after only an indeterminate reception in her own country. Now, all this was changed. Her recognition was whole-hearted, definite, exceptional. She gained self-confidence and was encouraged to persevere. She created image after image. She passed from the humble rose (*Spectre de la Rose*) to the exotic orchid of *Schéhérazade*, to the mournful asphodel of classic Hellas (*Echo*). I have dwelt at so much length on her *début* in Paris because this was her starting-point on that road to fame which, with sure and unerring footsteps, she has since followed.

FROM now onwards I do not propose to enumerate in chronological order the dancer's appearances abroad on European stages. Every year, before the War, she was in Paris, London, Monte Carlo; in Germany, Italy and South America. I will keep to important items in her *répertoire*, to the poetical images she actually created in the new choreography; that is to say, those on which her European fame is founded. But even an outline of her career must make mention of her success in London.

In a long article devoted to her, Mr. Gordon-Clifford writes:

'London has not yet ceased talking of Karsavina and her dancing; she is still the current topic of the season. We were shown in *Le Pavillon d'Armide* the extent of dramatic power, of tragic emotion, which this wonderful artist can express. Her art is rather akin to our own spirit. There is much naïve tenderness, much lovely purity, with fragrance and grace in her dancing. She has been called *the queen of modern dancing*. In some German theatres, the orchestras played the music of *Le Spectre de la Rose* by heart, while the musicians stood up and looked at the stage during the whole performance.

'At Covent Garden, at the end of the same ballet, she received from the gallery a bunch of roses with the touching inscription *To the Rose of Russia*. At the Grand Opéra in Paris, during an official charity performance that produced 100,000 francs, the ballet (*Le Spectre de la Rose*) had such an overwhelming success that, in response to the audience's repeated demand, the whole was given again from beginning to end—an unprecedented event in Paris. . . .'

Her visits abroad brought about a radical change in Karsavina's *répertoire*. In Petrograd, on the stage of the *Mariynsky Theatre*, she had been searching for herself. She had had at her disposal the immense lists of the old classical ballets by former masters, more especially by St. Leon and Marius Petipa. Karsavina's own appreciation has made us acquainted with the fundamental character of this type of ballet. It possessed an insignificant subject-matter drawn out to six or seven acts. It was composed of a series of dances, either classical or combined with the ' character ' dance, the whole being presented as a long and wearisome *divertissement* which, in detail, consisted of solos, *pas de deux*, *pas d'action*, for the leading dancer; marches, processions and waltzes for the *corps de ballet*;

lengthy pantomimic scenes, intended to rest both spectators and dancers ; and lastly, a happy apotheosis for all !

Karsavina has told us that it was this kind of production which the enterprise of Diaghileff brought to an inglorious finish. Petipa's old ballets had taught her to dance, had accustomed her to the stage, to plastic gymnastics, to endurance and to physical labour. Having mastered the entire technique of dancing, she was able to study in the new style—that of dancing closely allied to music, where every movement of the body corresponded to some phrase of melody and where the dance was not an isolated factor, but part and parcel of the dramatic situation. Through the new ballets, Karsavina had learned to invest her dancing with a true dramatic insight of the subject represented. Therefore, when after touring she returned to the old ballets of the St. Petersburg *répertoire*, she was able to present them in a new conception—to endow them with a new spirit. In this way the old school was not without its value to her, on account of the labour it had forced her to expend on the technical forms of dancing ; while the modern school gave her the advantage of acquiring dramatic idealisation, with the power to infuse artistry into her productions. Each was the complement of the other. A gifted artist was able to draw from both whatever was indispensable in either, thus individualising the various principles of choreography. Perhaps it is to this persistent effort in every direction of her creative work that we owe the wonderful dancer—Karsavina. . . .

She had had to create abroad a new *répertoire* no less extensive than that of the *Mariynsky Theatre*. It did not contain *seven* act ballets, with prologues and epilogues. For the most part the pieces were *one* act ballets, though the dances in them were none the less important on that account. An individualistic art gave incomparably more scope for study and development.

From the long list of ballets created abroad by Karsavina, it is difficult to decide which can be considered her masterpiece. To state that *Le Spectre de la Rose* is her greatest achievement is incorrect in view of its competitors. Who can forget *L'Oiseau de Feu—Petrouchka—Narcisse—Le Carnaval—Le Coq d'Or?* . . .

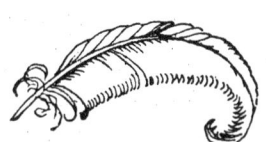

IT was in *Le Pavillon d'Armide* that Thamar Karsavina made her greatest impression on the Parisian public. In the enigmatic mystery of this tale—so entirely reminiscent of Hoffmann—reality and fantasy are blended in a wholly fanciful dream. The ballet reproduces the epoch of the Roi Soleil, and the costumes and decorations are in Louis XIV. style. The period is represented in all its ancient brilliancy; while the artists Alexander Benois, Fokine and Karsavina gave vivid life to a past epoch. In this ballet, the part of the *première danseuse* is largely one of dancing interest; besides being highly classical. In it I first saw Karsavina reveal one of her most valuable qualities, the true understanding of style, of the sentiment of the subject as interpreted by the dance.

It might be thought sufficient to dance a classical subject in a strictly classical manner; but such a capacity is possessed by any gifted *ballerina*. Karsavina achieved more. She so interpreted the classical elements of the ballet as to impart to her *rôle* the style as well as the spirit in which the authors had conceived it. As an artist enamoured of the epoch, she spiritualised her dancing in this ballet, transforming it into a living picture by Watteau or Boucher. Her dancing had the atmosphere of a capricious, captivating madrigal. The dance reflected subtlety of attitude, variety and richness of movement, and glowed with the brilliant colouring of a magnificent era. She was the queenly, legendary *Armide* seen among the splendours of a bygone century. For myself and many others accustomed to admire her in the purely classical productions of the old *répertoire* that had no style, it was a delightful surprise to watch her pursuing in the new ballet these fresh effects of style. I understood that for the first time she had discovered her real vocation and that every day her genius was acquiring depth and artistry.

Les Sylphides, in which Karsavina appeared on the same occasion, is essentially a dancing ballet, without any literary subject. It may be called dancing for the sake of dancing. Chopin's melodies are interpreted by plastic movements. It is not even a picture; rather is it a synthetic expression of the elements of romanticism. A melody of Chopin, long white skirts, a simple *bandeau* and a pensive brow; a dance beneath the moon, the atmosphere of the Thirties, a dreamy mood—who can recognise the capricious Karsavina of the XVII. century *Armide?* It is the poetical dream of a spring night, when among the moonbeams, an ethereal sylph descends to that earth which she scarcely touches with her feet. Infinite delicacy of perception is shown by her manner of interpreting a style, the lines and features of which are invisible to the average spectator and which her talent discovers by means of some unerring instinct of her own. It is these lines and features that in some mysterious way compose the atmosphere that is style!

Another of her creations in the romantic manner, at the same period, was *Columbine* in Schumann's *Carnaval*. Here, if I may so express myself, the interpretation is in a totally different key. In *Les Sylphides* we saw a sad fantasy, transparent and fragrant as a moonlit night in early summer, a tender song without words, a lyrical expression of melancholy dreams. In *Le Carnaval* we are present at a joyous festival on an eve full of gaiety, of picturesque incident, love and jealousy, intrigue, disappointment and laughter—songs too, but sung joyfully, in a spirit of reciprocation—of a fancy-dress ball. Again, the essence of this ballet is romanticism. There is no realistic drama; only sketches, glimpses, as it were, of human passion displayed in a number of jovial adventures of which we see only the humorous summary.

Carnaval is the most individualistic of all Schumann's compositions. It is the one most closely united to his own mentality and connected with episodes in his own life. These short musical expressions of the poet's soul, his vivid and harmonious movements, his wealth of ideas had awakened the admiration of two great *virtuosi* of the period—Clara Wieck and Franz Liszt. And Karsavina might have been born during the years of Schumann's romanticism, so well has she identified herself with the conventional grace and hyper-sensibility of a century of dreamy sadness. There is no false note in her execution of the ballet. The fine irony and tender smiles of Schumann's *Carnaval* are blended in her dancing into plastic visions set in an atmosphere of melody.

Karsavina's performance of *Le Carnaval* in Paris, and later in St. Petersburg, inspired poets as well as painters. Of the former, D. Krachkovsky, in his volume entitled *Palette*, has dedicated two sonnets—*Les Deux Sonnets de l'Amoureux de Columbine*—to the *ballerina* who fascinated him. In one he testifies that as *Columbine*, ' Karsavina has stepped down from a faded picture of the Thirties!' ... ' The heroine of this romantic epoch had sad eyes.' ... ' Yes, truly Karsavina is a Queen of Columbines.' ...

A sequel to *Le Carnaval* was the small ballet *Papillons* in which Fokine was not so successful. It is a far-fetched epilogue to its inspired original. It appeared much later and was but a pale copy. The part of the *Young Girl* is again a purely dancing one, which, in spite of its choregraphic difficulties, Karsavina performed with purely classical technique. But neither the dance nor the *rôle* added a single leaf to the wreath of fame crowning her at the moment.

Before we leave the romantic period with its delicate style—the epoch of Taglioni—a few words may be said concerning the early Victorian maiden in *Le Spectre de la Rose*. In this part Karsavina took every great town in Europe by storm. The music of this ballet is Weber's *Invitation à la Valse*. From the choregraphic point of view it is a classical dance, conceived in the simple and noble style of the romantic period. The subject is a girl's dream after a ball. She returns, full of naïve and innocent fancies, to her bedroom, and overtired, falls asleep without undressing, while still clasping in her hands the rose given to her by her lover. The rising moon can be seen through the big French windows that open upon a mysterious park. All at once the flower is transformed into a youth—a rose-like vision—who draws her into a whirling dance. Then the vision floats through the window and disappears into the garden; while the maiden falls exhausted into a chair. She awakes. At her feet lies a faded rose. That is all. . . .

The simplicity of the music, choregraphy and poetry may, rendered in dry words, produce scant interest, but in reality, as executed by Nijinsky and Karsavina, the dance is resplendent, dazzling in its beauty; while music, choregraphy, subject, decorations and costumes (Bakst) all take their place in one artistic whole. There is nothing superfluous in this ballet. Everything is fragrant with subtle and delicate charm. It is most difficult to discriminate between reality and fantasy. Karsavina creates an image of such loveliness that it is not easy to imagine anything more perfect. The ballet contains no pantomime and no dramatic subject. Like *Sylphides*, it is an apotheosis of dancing. It is ripe with the pure romantic classicism with which Maria Taglioni conquered Europe and America.

'Nowhere,' says the art critic Alexander Benois, ' has Karsavina created so perfect an image of bashful, girlish grace—at once pure and passionate—as in this unusual *rôle* of a half-sleeping, half-waking

girl.' Here Karsavina has attained an extraordinarily high level of creative power—perhaps I should say of style.

Her *Armide* is composed after a pretentiously artificial fashion in the lofty manner of the Roi Soleil; a manner absolutely opposed to the pensive, naïve methods of the romantic school. One might easily imagine that two different performers were required for these interpretations. I have purposely placed side by side in this chapter the two periods of Louis XIV. and 1830 in order to show to what degree Karsavina has been able to represent the two methods and the remarkable scope she enjoys in reincarnation. Down to the minutest detail, she assimilates the lines, features, colours and expressions, which, duly co-ordinated and combined, compose, as I have said, the style atmosphere.

There are dancers who imagine that a ballet is no more than a ballet, that classicism is just classicism, that a dance to be classic must be executed as such, according to strict rule and custom. But if there is no reciprocity between art and form, no blending of artistic features with plastic beauty of attitude; if there is no general idea in a dance beyond dancing, it can never be a perfectly artistic creation. Gymnastics, carried to a degree of virtuosity, and *pointes*, even if steel-like, are insufficient in themselves. Similarly technique can exist without creation, and dancing without art. Only the dancer who understands the beauty of the human body in movement and immobility, and in the suspense that lies between, is able to reach in her dancing the domain of the art creative. Karsavina is such a dancer. She feels instinctively the difference between artistic classicism and classical routine.

THE return from the romantic manner of the XIX. century to the ancient style is even more abrupt than the transition from the pompous methods of *Armide* to the simpler and nobler attributes of *Les Sylphides* and *Le Carnaval*. But Karsavina's appearance in Fokine's Greek ballets was not unexpected. Before touring abroad, she had already danced in *Eunice*, the first of Fokine's attempts in the direction of the antique. It has been suggested that the essay was only half successful, for the new interpretation, while attempting to reproduce the ancient period, was still prone to resemble the pseudo-antiques of the old ballet; the young author had not succeeded yet in freeing himself entirely from its influence, a fact particularly noticeable in the grouping and stage ensemble which still showed relationship to the so-called *ballabille* ballets of Petipa. To avoid repetition I will not return to this subject.

At any rate these reminiscences had disappeared from *Daphnis et Chloë*, and especially from *Narcisse*. The new ideals which sought to represent ancient Greek sculpture and ceramics had triumphed. It was Isadora Duncan who had conceived them with a view to the renaissance of the ballet.

Now everything hopelessly old-fashioned had combated Isadora Duncan in her pathetic artistic campaign. I do not speak so much of the critics who at the time were on Petipa's side and who would see no farther than the enchanted circle of his ballets, for it was their sectarian faith that to deviate in the slightest from tradition was to betray the 'great laws.' It was sadder to see the hostility shown by the dancers themselves. One after another, either in writing or in words, condemned Isadora Duncan's influence as something satanic. . . . However, to give here a complete picture of the struggle would be to travel too far afield.

Karsavina never belonged to the groups of the 'Old Believers.' . . .

Her keen and bright intelligence, ever seeking novelty in art, at once led her to the new movement. To me, the *rôle* of the nymph *Echo* in the ballet *Narcisse*—music by Tcherepnine, decorations and costumes by Bakst—was one of the best pictures Karsavina ever created. And I was not alone in thinking so; because all the critics, foreign as well as Russian, who were present at that performance were equally impressed by her dancing.

I will extract another passage from A. Benois where he deals with Karsavina as *Echo*. I have to speak so highly of Karsavina in my book and praise her creative work so immeasurably, that in order to avoid a suspicion of partiality, I feel obliged from time to time to quote the opinion of others.

A. Benois is a most straightforward critic. He is incapable of awarding exaggerated panegyric to any one, merely for the sake of being amiable. ' Both Karsavina and Nijinsky, have given proofs of real courage by accepting difficult and ungrateful *rôles*. Yet from beginning to end, both were beautiful and dramatic.

' Karsavina astonished me. I had believed her a good dancer, a sympathetic and conscientious artist, but I never expected of her either the courage to dance the part of this god-like being persecuted by ill fate, or the wonderful success which she achieved.

' Karsavina is a tender *Giselle*, a lovely *Armide*, an amusing *Ballerine* (in *Petrouchka*); but here she has succeeded in imposing on her *rôle* a character of severe, unconventional classicism. Her imitation of the gestures of *Narcissus*, her malediction and her attempts to restore him to life, are movements which lift her above the level of a charming and graceful dancer to that of a great actress.'

Yes, it may be definitely stated that Karsavina was wonderful in that exceedingly difficult part of a nymph who sacrifices herself and is repudiated by the Gods.

To do justice to the dancer of *Echo*, the full dramatic force of the ballet must be understood. An ancient myth, far estranged from modern life, is made to appear singularly near and human to the spectator. The tale is full of sadness; its conclusion mournful to a degree; and the nymph's despair unfathomable. The intense melancholy of a performance achieved with remarkable simplicity and even economy of gesture, seemed to bridge the space between the past and the present.

In representing the part, Karsavina touchingly depicted the poignant picture of a woman's grief. In addition to this she employed that inherent sense of beauty attributed to the ancient Greeks and which is delineated so artistically on their vases; the expressive eyes, the shrinking form, even the mournful purple tunic. With all this artistry, there was a moderation, a limitation of pose and gesture, a symbolic rendering of the grief naturally expressed by covering the head to hide the stricken features, a reserve which far from marring the beauty of the human face and body, enhances it in the interpretation of the tragic emotions.

By some mysterious mental process Karsavina succeeded in preserving intact the rich colour of the tragedy and in imparting to her audience a vivid sensation of its truth. I consider *Echo* her first great achievement in the art of mime.

The second part of the ballet consists of pantomime without much dancing. There is a long portrayal of the betrayed nymph's despair, an achievement which might have given rise to apprehension, since the ballet was to be presented to a Parisian public. However, Karsavina's evident love of the *rôle*, made plain by her execution of it and the ever-recurring brilliance she infused into the course of its creation, were such that it was just these long expositions—which might easily have proved monotonous—that engaged the public's attention and won its admiration.

The part of *Chloë* in the ballet *Daphnis et Chloë* by M. Ravel—decorations and costumes by Bakst—afforded another opportunity for Karsavina's gifts. The theme is very similar to that of *Narcisse*. The subject is taken from the story of Longus. Its tender poetry produces the impression of a *pastorale*, simple in form and delicate in detail. The artistic idea is naïve, but sincere. In this ballet Fokine seems to have wished to prove his versatility as a *maître-de-ballet*. Each dance has its own *motif*. That of *Chloë* is characterised by a delicate and lyric sadness. That of the two principals together is light and graceful, reminiscent of a pencil sketch. Karsavina is an ideal *Chloë*. She is imbued with the spirit of the Greek tale and dances with the pastoral simplicity of ancient times. Her tender and unaffected portrayal of the chaste *Chloë* is inferior in nothing to the mournful and lofty image she evokes of the nymph *Echo*. To complete the picture, I will mention a third production, *Midas* (music by Steinberg), which for some reason left no lasting trace in Diaghileff's *répertoire*. It appears to have been too insignificant to add materially to Karsavina's fame as a dancer.

WE have now seen Karsavina in the realm of ancient myths. With the aid of pantomime, movement and gesture, she has eloquently told the tale of a highly cultured people and brought before us the vivid images of a far-away legendary period. We will now judge how she relates Russian tales and how she illustrates our national folk-lore.

Of this group, she has created three *rôles*, in the ballets *L'Oiseau de Feu*, *Le Coq d'Or* and *Petrouchka*; the first two are tales of the people, the third—according to A. Benois' expression—*a tale of the street*.

The production of *L'Oiseau de Feu* marks the first complete attempt to bring a Russian popular myth on to the choreographic stage. There had been previous essays, *Le Petit Cheval Bossu*, *Le Poisson d'Or*, and, perhaps, a few others. But the attempt had been made with inadequate means. The ballets had a senseless subject-matter, second-rate music and only the usual stage choreography, to which was added a few pseudo-national dances. The compositions were lacking in taste, in style and in true national character. They gave an impression of vulgarity. Were it not for the evident belief of their authors that Russian folk-lore cannot be represented in any other way, the style might be referred to as a merely stupid misconception of Russian fairy tales. For a long time this belief actually existed among the Russian public, until *L'Oiseau de Feu* proved that Russian myths were peculiarly adaptable to choreographic production.

A ' Girl King,' clad in a short gauze skirt and wearing pink ballet shoes, dancing *sur les pointes*, makes a Russian ballet no less nonsensical than a *Minuet de la Cour* danced in a Russian *sarafan*. Yet for a long while nobody seemed to notice this.

Even in *L'Oiseau de Feu*, despite Stravinsky's delightful music, which had its place on the programmes of symphony concerts, there remained numerous defects due to its being the first genuine production in ballet form of a Russian popular tale. But on the whole it had the required elements on which to base a production that was both artistic and original. Its success was due to Karsavina who, undaunted by its difficult technique, created the principal part.

In the fairy dress of the *Bird of Fire*, the fluttering gestures of the dancer's arms, her wonderful suggestion of flying, her emotional dance when she finds herself in the power of *Ivan the Tzarevitch*, and the slow, smooth movement which puts to sleep the entire kingdom of *Kostcheï*, Karsavina was the true incarnation of a myth, the materialised image of a fictitious world. Her dancing was persuasively full of life, though not as a personification of everyday existence. It figured a world beyond our own. It threw into bold relief the dazzling richness of colouring of this Phœnix of Russian folk-lore, a bird of golden plumage and fiery, vari-coloured rays. Nevertheless, the obstacles of technique, with its many forms, outlines and virtuosities, remained a sealed book to the audience. Karsavina was careful to conceal the hard work required by the *rôle*. She let the public see only the result. The Terpsichorean image evoked might have been improvised on the stage in a moment of inspiration. Only a true artist can create in this way. When listening to a musical symphony which induces artistic emotions of a high order, one is apt to forget the material labour accomplished by the composer in the pages he has covered with innumerable musical signs. Only an expert could have seen through the close network of movement, posture, technique and tricks of virtuosity, in which the choregraphy of *L'Oiseau de Feu* abounds. Karsavina transformed the whole into a fairy revel and thereby earned the entire admiration of the audience. Among French critics, this performance created a feeling almost of wonder. One wrote, ' The dancer is of quite exceptional value. Her skill is a riddle. To an acrobatic suppleness she adds the impression of a goddess-like aloofness from everything earthly. Out of a storm a fairy bird drops from the far-distant land of fantasy.'

Personally, I thought her still more astonishing as the *Queen of Shemâkhan* in *Le Coq d'Or* of Rimsky-Korsakoff. This beautiful posthumous work of the Russian composer was forbidden at first in Russia, and later only allowed to appear with a number of ridiculous cuts and alterations by the Censor. Diaghileff presented it for the first time in its entirety at the *Théâtre des Champs-Elysées*, Paris, in June, 1914.

The production of the opera aroused a fierce polemic in the Press owing to the daring originality of the theme. Each *rôle* was allocated at the same time to two performers, one vocal and one choregraphic. While the vocal part was taken by a singer placed among other musical performers all clothed alike and seated on tribunes at both sides of the stage, the same *rôle* was acted chore-

graphically by a dancer. Thus the part of *King Dodon* was sung in the wings by a vocalist and at the same time mimed on the stage by a dancer. The *rôle* of the *Queen of Shemâkhan* was sung by Madame Dobrovolskaïa and danced by Karsavina. The same arrangement held good for the choruses.

In this production rhythm was, as it were, set apart as an independent creation. The idea seems to have been the materialisation of the soul of the musical work. The outlines of the dancers' movements corresponded to the outlines of the melody. Each movement answered to a note. The musical partition was set in choreography and its sounds made incarnate in plastic forms. The close blending of music and movement produced complete illusion. Karsavina appeared to be singing herself. There was something mystical both in the division and in the union. And Karsavina's fascinating image as the *Queen of Shemâkhan* was another fairy vision, a dream translated into rhythm. Whatever of mystery and Eastern lyrical sentiment Rimsky-Korsakoff had thrown into his opera was more than adequately rendered by her pantomime and dancing. She grasped at the same time the style of the fantasy and the style of the music.

Is it possible to describe melody ? It must be heard. Can dancing be explained ? It must be seen. What does a reader understand when told that an adagio in a major key of one of Beethoven's sonatas contains three flats and that the time is $\frac{9}{8}$; further, that there are such and such notes, such and such signs in the first measure ? It is just as useless to attempt to explain to him that, in a particular ballet, a dancer executed an *entrechat*, a *pirouette*, a *pas de basque*, a *saut de chat*, or a *rond de jambe*. Music must be heard, dancing watched. That is the reason why, in speaking of the great ballerina's art, I am endeavouring to analyse its substance, its spirit and its style, without touching on its material technique. Some critics have attempted to do this, have described step by step, in technical terms, the execution of a *variation*. Their efforts were ridiculed. In the same way, whoever has seen Karsavina in the *rôle* of the *Queen of Shemâkhan* will never forget the artistic emotions experienced ; so those who have not seen her, will obtain no impression of value from any mere description of her dancing.

In *Petrouchka*, Karsavina took the part of the *Ballerine*. As I have mentioned already, her principal collaborator in the ballet has called it **a tale of the street**.

With all its simplicity of design, the subject is a cryptic one from the point of view of psychology. *Petrouchka*, the *Ballerine* and the *Moor* are marionettes in whom an unseen spectator has guessed the existence of a soul. Somewhere behind, the dolls live in a box lined with bright-flowered wallpaper. This box is their home and in it takes place, unknown to the merry drunken audience, an intimate drama.

The marionettes are put through their performances before the public by a conjuror and charlatan. They are dolls, with expressionless wooden faces and mechanical movements; but at home in their box, which the imagination of the spectator changes into a room, they become, if not real people, at least half-human beings of primitive, rudimentary passions simplified to the utmost degree.

The Moor loves the Ballerine, who is also beloved of Petrouchka, who in turn is jealous of the Moor. The Ballerine flirts with the Moor and is afraid both of him and Petrouchka. The Moor kills Petrouchka. That is all. Perhaps it is of the ' soul of things,' of Maeterlinck, of Andersen. Nevertheless a weird mysticism emanates from this drama of dolls. The mysticism is mingled with symbolism. Petrouchka, when his body is rent by the Moor, appears to be only a doll stuffed with sawdust. The Guard ascertains this, and yet his proprietor suddenly sees him alive again on his stage and flees in terror. Petrouchka's immortality is the immortality of the Russian people's tales. . . .

To grasp the indefinable bond between the mysterious reality and the mystic fantasy of this *rôle* of the *Ballerine*, the artist must be extremely sensitive and possess a subtle comprehension of psychology.

' All this *rôle*,' writes Alexander Benois of Nijinsky in the part of Petrouchka, ' consists in the interpretation of a weak, nervous character, whose efforts to gain personal happiness and dignity are ineffective. It is written in a minor key—in a depressed, neurasthenic fashion. The character is doomed to lasting grief, interrupted only by deceptive outbursts of joy, followed by stupefied despair. . . . There are no turns, no embellishments, nothing to give the comforting idea of " pleasing the audience." '

Exactly the same may be said of Karsavina as the *Ballerine*. In the ballet sense of the word the part scarcely contains a dance. Costume and make-up are those of a coarse doll; while her love affair with the black man is more comical than appealing. But she never forgets her dollship and, with allusiveness and simplified utterance of feeling, she reaches the heart of the spectator.

Benois describes her thus—' In taking the silly *rôle* of the doll in *Petrouchka*, Karsavina once again proves her artistic interest in her task. In the special ballet sense of the words, no such thing as an " ungrateful task " exists for her. Art is always there to console her. In spite of the accentuated silliness of the part, and without in any way modifying it, she succeeded in being delightful in it.'

Yes, she was a sweet, touching and amusing doll, besides being a provokingly frivolous woman, whose stupidity may be regarded as the natural attribute of her doll's soul. When wound up by her proprietor, the conjuror, to twirl before the drunken carnival crowd, she is a genuine doll-marionette; yet how like a woman, when dancing with the trumpet, she strives, silly as she is, to fascinate the terrible Moor, who plays with her just as he has been playing with his cocoanut, mistaking it for a mystic deity.

It is no paradox to say that the dancer's art is more rigorous than that of the actress. In the real drama the actor has at his disposal not only mimic and plastic gesture, but also speech, that all-powerful instrument of human thought and feeling. The dancer does not possess this instrument but is restricted to the silent elements of motion and pantomime. Therefore to render silence as expressive as words is a gift of very exceptional power. Yet, granted the plastic genius of Karsavina and Nijinsky, it is possible, as Alexander Benois says, *to interpret by means of the ballet a drama, which in the form of opera or tragedy, could never be performed!* . . .

IN the domain of human intelligence and of the aspirations of the human soul, there are many unconscious images and vague emotions which cannot be rendered effectively in speech. Lermontoff points out the difficulty of describing the battle of thought in cold words. Tutchev says—*A spoken thought is a lie.*

In the spirit is a silence stronger than words—a subconscious or unconscious yearning of the mind for fuller expression. Mysterious fragments of distant and elusive thought, many obscure and harassing emotions, wreathe and drift like clouds, and like them evoke images of fantastic castles which in turn fall to ruins, to change again to the incongruous shape of a monstrous, fanciful beast. Such are the workings of dreams and unexpressed feelings in the depths of the human mind; dreams and feelings which vainly seek expression either in sculpture, painting, drama or literature. For emotion belongs to music. It is music that gives shape to those fleecy cloud-shapes, advancing, growing, melting, and dispersing only to form again. Human speech can take little account of them. Only musically, will they unfold in the abodes of our imagination, beating in unison with it. They are the shadows and secrets of human emotion.

Rhythm is the soul of music. In it fancy and desire find their full expression. Music and dancing, combined and indivisible, closely united since the beginning, dutifully comply with the great world principle of rhythm. And may it not be that it was rhythm and dancing between them evoked music? May not that be why the realm of music has always been that of dancing—why the strange excitement of emotion has always been that especially attributable to the rhythmic cults? There is no doubt whatever that melody in combination with pantomime has produced rhythmo-plastic forms and movements unattainable by more material forms of art.

The statue's plastic shapes are immobile. In a picture the harmony of colour is immutable; while the lyrics of prose and poetry are imprisoned for ever in the fetters of speech. When stone, paint and words have exhausted their means of expression then music begins—the song without words and independent of matter, corresponding to the ideal domain of the spirit which expresses the whole joy of living. Music and dancing, once a single art, now jointly conform to the laws of rhythm in providing an emotional drama which is the highest known to mankind.

If the dancer's soul is sensitive and responsive to the call of emotion and rhythm, then a dancer can be a great artist. If the dancer's soul strives toward true union with music, then the dance can create images without words, pure visions of rhythmo-plastic form full of lyrical emotion.

To such a dancer, the style or period matters little. It may be one of romanticism, of Greek mythology, of Russian folk-lore, or of Orientalism.

Karsavina is such a dancer. Whether in the brilliant and gorgeous epoch of Louis XIV., in the simple sphere of pensive romanticism, in ancient myth, in Russian fairy tale or in the half-fantastic, half-realistic story of street, she is a great artist, excelling in all styles, deficient in none.

KARSAVINA has created another style of choregraphic production to which I have not yet referred, that is to say, the ballets in the Eastern manner. And it is perhaps here that while her *répertoire* is richest in images, her transitions have been most marked.

The early Victorian maiden dreaming in the moonlight, her lover's rose in her hand, becomes the passionate *odalisque* surrendering with animal passion to the amorous caresses of a negro. The tender, ethereal *Sylphide* changes in another ballet to the cruel, sadist and deeply-suffering *Salome*. It is a mystery of genius. It is the art of personification. In some manner incomprehensible to us the spiritual organisation of talent becomes impregnated with the atmosphere of the composition which it is destined to interpret. ... The fragrant air of a spring night penetrating the room of the early Victorian maiden, and the heavy perfume of Eastern scents pervading the close atmosphere of the *harêm*, both give to the imagination of the artist the required tone for a character's interpretation. To touch the pedal of a harp is to change the key. In a great talent there is a succession of such pedals, pressure on any one of which has a similar effect; and the artist must conform to the key.

We have seen Karsavina as *Columbine*, as the maiden with the rose, as a *Sylphide*. In all these *rôles* she was tender, romantic, poetical. But now we have to see her as the Shah's sultana, the submissive *Zobeide*; and it would appear as though all at once, the indolence, the careless unconcern, the voluptuousness of the East had entered her blood. As she reclines on the cushions of the *harêm*, no glimmer of expression illumines her dark eyes. She is a bewitchingly beautiful creature in whom the perfumed, monotonous, spiritless existence of the *harêm*—with its splashing fountains, brutal conditions and dull boredom—has eradicated every spark of soul.

Then the Shah departs. . . .

His wives awake from their lethargy. . . .

When the negroes enter, these Eastern houris spring forward to meet them, like lust-maddened beasts.

In this scene Karsavina is wonderful.

She knows the fine limit that divides coarse realism from artistic portrayal. Her great eyes are aflame with unrestrained passion; which is perhaps not so much a desire of the flesh as an angry protest against slavery. Her supple body writhes feverishly in the negro's arms. It is the moment of her triumph. With her garments, with the fetters of the zenana, she throws aside the humility of the slave. The jealous eye of a morose master, the cold glances of sexless eunuchs are forgotten. She is a serf no more. She is free. It is her festival, her recompense, her vengeance. She treads out her pleasure to the end. Her soul has been stupefied and her body made wanton by bondage. The spirit of lust conquers and a wild orgy of passion ensues.

Suddenly, blood and death bring this orgy to an abrupt termination.

The quick transition from an ecstasy of the flesh to the vision of an inevitable death is expressed so completely by the dancer that those who have seen her representation only once, are unlikely ever to forget the supreme tragedy of that moment. The dark eyes excited with wine, dancing and fierce desire, are ablaze with triumph —suddenly they are filled with terror. The sultana has not realised exactly what has happened; but the dead bodies and streams of blood which stain the floor show that the dreadful and the inevitable have come to pass. With the fatalism of the Oriental woman, she regains her self-control and stands proudly before her lord. She

knows the punishment of her crime, but she regrets nothing. She understands she is to die and she kills herself with the haughty dignity of the revolted slave, who neither expects nor desires pardon. Perhaps it is still within her reach, but she rejects it with all the arrogance of her unrepentant soul.

Fokine's masterpiece *Schéhérazade* has afforded Karsavina full opportunities for revealing her great histrionic gifts. It is an exceptionally true interpretation of the East, one which her genius has grasped instinctively.

Islamei is another ballet by Fokine which deals with almost an identical subject. It was never produced abroad, and in St. Petersburg, only at the *Mariynsky Theatre*. I mention it in order to give a complete account of Karsavina's Eastern representations. As is generally the case with copies, this ballet is greatly inferior to its original. Why Fokine should have chosen a mere variation of a theme that had made him famous, it is difficult to understand. Perhaps it was because of the impossibility of producing *Schéhérazade* before a St. Petersburg public. If so, he desired to produce at least something similar. *Islamei* is shorter than *Schéhérazade*, the action developing more quickly. It is scarcely more than a sketch, with a single episode, which is the culminating point of the ballet. No particular development leads up to the climax, which gives an odd impression of abruptness. Karsavina's *rôle* is too limited. It is devoid of incident and overwhelmed by the too brilliant and confusing *ensemble* that surrounds her. Her part is not sufficiently conspicuous. The background overwhelms the picture. The eye is dazzled by a surfeit of colouring in the decoration and the costumes. Not only is the *rôle* too slight, but its lights and shadows are too inharmonious.

Karsavina appeared again as a tragic Eastern woman in another of Fokine's ballets, *Thamar*, a subtle production inspired by Balakireff's symphonic poem, to the spirit of which it corresponds. It also contains an orgy, though of a different kind. It occurs among men and has nothing to do with the episodes of the *harêm*. It is characterised by the reserve habitual to the Caucasian mountain tribes. Karsavina is again the centre of a production which revolves about her. Without employing melodramatic effect or cheap tragedy, and while preserving a wonderful economy of gesture, as well as of reserve in movement, she reveals in her pantomime immense strength of character. The presence of the mysterious *Thamar*, fascinating and morose, the elusive sphinx of the legend, is put clearly before the spectator. At moments the dancer reaches vertiginous heights of artistic creation. Her success in the *rôle* is most remarkable.

In *The Tragedy of Salome*, produced by Romanoff to the music of the French composer Florent Schmitt, Karsavina's *rôle*, in spite of the tragic subject, lacks life and conviction. The part does not render at all clear the character of the girl who bewitched Herod with her dancing. Salome is no longer of this earth. She is a shade expiating her sin in unknown spheres. She is a spirit astray in the eternal and limitless regions of ether, in the starry fields of inter-planetary space, which we cannot reach even in our imagination.

As a meteor, she roams, haunted, terror-stricken by the perpetual vision of the Baptist's head. Sometimes she descends from these unsubstantial heights to witness the horrible group of executioners who have beheaded the victim of her terrible dance, while the Head, dread symbol, is always with her.

She remembers the far-off past, which awakens the longing for dancing. Before the awful Head, she treads out her sadist theme, as one deprived of thought and will, as though obeying an inner command which demands the dance as an expiation. From the choregraphic point of view, this is a long and difficult performance. The production is symbolic, with a tendency to philosophy. It is rather tedious. Karsavina performs the arduous *rôle* well. She gives the part its proper character of aloofness, of a reflected reminiscence. In her figure and movements there is something weird, emblematic of despair and horror.

From the tragic Eastern images Karsavina has made incarnate, that of *Ta-Hor* in *Une Nuit d'Egypte* must not be omitted. This ballet is almost free from ancient convention. It contains nothing in the manner of the old ballet. The name even, of ballet, is incorrect for it. Instead, an art is introduced which expresses the whole complex psychology of life. It is rather a drama without words, in which dancing enters as an element in the composition, but not the most important one. The principal component is the spirit of the artist *maître-de-ballet* who creates this vision of a warm Egyptian night. In this tale the rhythm of life and feeling has been understood. This is the reason why the dancer's plastic art proves once more the synthesis of both. As Fokine is in his drama, so is Karsavina in her dancing. Both understand the rhythm of form and feeling. She is again the Eastern slave, but not the slave-*odalisque* of *Schéhérazade* or *Islamei* with a soul made dissolute by the enervating air of the *harêm*. She has grown in liberty and possesses a loving, passionate heart. She is ready to revolt openly against her soul's slavery; to struggle with the powerful will, robbing her, for a moment's lascivious caprice, of a whole life's joy. She gives her very true expression to the psychology of such moments. She reveals the hidden rhythm of the half-mythical, half-mystic East, fascinating us with its richness of colour, its esotericism, and, at the same time, its nearness.

The ballet concludes with the episode in which the poor woman —forsaken by all, mocked in her love, insulted in her pride, overpowered by grief—sobs despairingly over the body of *Amoûn*, who has paid with his life for a fleeting moment of ecstasy. This *rôle* acquires through Karsavina's masterly execution a most powerful and dramatic significance.

To complete the list of Karsavina's Eastern creations, I must mention the Buddhist girl from whom her betrothed, who is to become a Brahmin, is taken away. In this *rôle*, through no fault of her own, the dancer has achieved but little. *Le Dieu Bleu* is a failure in every sense of the word—in subject, in musical composition, in *decor* and in stage management. Its one redeeming feature is Fokine's choregraphy. He is a poet either of subtle, plastic expression or of wild, bacchic excess. He either creates lyrical dramas, as in the case of *Le Spectre de la Rose* and *Les Sylphides*, or is carried away by an almost delirious fantasy, as in his numerous bacchanals, which attain such extraordinary swing and rhythm. Before this insignificant subject and uninteresting music he seems to have hesitated and to have concentrated his powers upon ethnographical Hindu plasticism. Much erudition, a thorough study of documents and a very considerable artistic instinct are to be felt in this translation of representative Hindu iconography into the dynamics of the dance. But that is all. There is present neither real life nor true artistic inspiration.

Obviously the performers cannot have been inspired by either the author or the composer. Still, Karsavina makes the most of the part of the Buddhist girl. The scene of the parting with her lover is touching, but there remains nothing for her to do afterwards. The succeeding scenes convey only a false impression of gilded splendour. She is surrounded by red, black and gold monsters, which seem to have escaped from some Marigny revue, on a tour to the *Chatelet!* . . . It is easy to understand that a *rôle* like this added nothing to the dancer's fame. It passed as a merely chance episode to disappear without a trace.

Till now, Karsavina has been seen in Fokine's numerous productions; that is to say, in the new ballet that took the place of Petipa's classical period. In the book *Le Ballet Contemporain*[1] I have done my best to follow this movement from its origin and to assign to it its correct place in the evolution of choreography. I need not refer to the matter again here. I will only say that Nijinsky, assisted in his enterprise by Diaghileff, undertook a still further development of the ballet. He endeavoured to create something that would be to Fokine what Fokine was to Petipa. Nijinsky conceived and produced three ballets which were to be entirely new—*L'Après Midi d'un Faune*, *Le Sacre du Printemps*, and *Jeux*. In all of these reproductions dancing was entirely eliminated. In *L'Après Midi d'un Faune* he gave the all but statuesque plasticity of an ancient bas relief. In *Le Sacre du Printemps* there are primitive, archaic, rudimentary movements which suggest a dance of rustics. Lastly, in *Jeux*, we see a series of quasi-athletic movements and postures, all rigidly conventionalised and studied. On the programme the production bore the sub-title '*Poëme Dansée*.'

In the first two of these Karsavina took no part. But in *Jeux*, she and L. Schollar represented girls playing tennis. The subject of the ballet is simplicity itself.

The scene is a park, lighted with electric lanterns, which illuminate the approaching semi-darkness of twilight. From away behind the trees falls a tennis ball struck by distant players. A youth and two little girls in tennis costume come running into the park to look for the ball. The fun of searching in the green grass amuses them, and they start a game of hide-and-seek on their own

---

[1] Svétlov (V.) *Le Ballet Contemporain*, Société R. Golicke et A. Willborg, *St. Petersburg*, 1912. There is also a French edition translated by *M. D. Calvocoressi*, Brunoff, *Paris*, 1912.

account. They chase one another, quarrel, sulk without reason, and, I believe, forget the ball.

The approaching night is heavy with the perfume of flowers falling asleep in the garden. The fantastic light of the electric lanterns against the darkening sky conveys the impression of fairyland, while the instinctive feeling of spring awakens in the young people an attraction for each other. They embrace and kiss, exciting each other's jealousy in turn. Theirs is a dangerous age. But another ball, hit by a mischievous or careless player, disturbs this spring-like fascination of love's young dream. Anxious and afraid, the children disappear in the depths of the park. That is the subject—poetic, fascinating in its simple psychology—a somewhat insignificant composition, brief and without analysis of character; but graceful, elegant and naïve.

Parisian critics have spoken of the pornography contained in this production. But I categorically protest against the accusation. Although I went to the theatre quite expecting to see that something of which the papers had complained, I did not detect the slightest pornographic allusion at any point of the performance. What is called an 'evil mind' can, of course, see pornography in the fact that two little girls kiss each other, and kiss the boy. But in our time such prudery is merely repulsive. It is unnatural and hypocritical.

I have said that there was no question of choregraphy in this ballet. The production is composed in the grotesque fashion made familiar by English illustrators. It is full of childish laughter, and is amusing from beginning to end. The rapid sequence of jealousy, tears and love, the steps taken half on tip-toe, the leaps among the flowers, are all droll. The capital error in the choregraphic stage-management of the ballet is the conventional, doll-like effect of contorted hands and bent heads, with the lack of all mimetic expression. There is no excuse for such defects of style in a lifelike production.

The suggestion has been advanced that Nijinsky hoped to present the spectator with a synthesis of twentieth-century movement; a vague, mistaken idea, for it is just in this far-fetched attempt that *Jeux* fails. French criticism also reproached the management with the introduction of Karsavina and Schollar in such a misconception. 'The most plastic and graceful of our dancers,' they said, ' are out of place in deformed attitudes, purposely made unnatural.' And it is unquestionably true that *Jeux* would have been of far greater artistic consequence had the little girls who played tennis and love-making been allowed to remain children, instead of queerly conventionalised dolls.

Nevertheless, clad in their white frocks and silhouetted against the green background of the park, Karsavina and Schollar are fascinating enough for the artificialities of the *mise en scène* to be quickly forgotten. Again, Nijinsky is wonderful in his effects of flying and leaping. But at one time it seemed possible that the stage-manager in him might kill the dancer who justly delights all Europe. The score which Debussy wrote specially for this ballet is both charming and delicate. It has nothing in common with the trite *poëmes dansées* of the days of Graziella and Paquerette. The orchestration is brilliant. The lover of sentimental dance melodies may not find much to admire, for the Debussy of *L'Après Midi d'un Faune* is no longer here. It is the Debussy of *Pélleas et Mélisande* who has seized a moment of leisure in which to set to music a graceful and polished scrap of pleasantry.

At this point it may be well to bring to a conclusion the narrative of Karsavina's visits abroad—that portion of her career which, more than any other, constitutes her claim to celebrity. Paris, London, Buenos Ayres, with many other towns in Europe and America, had been charmed by her dancing. Her position was secure. Portraits of the famous dancer adorned the periodicals of the whole world. Innumerable notes and reviews attested her popularity, and even fame. Numerous books were written in her praise. Well-known painters made pictures of her. For her, authors contrived new ballets, for which composers wrote new music. She was the most fashionable dancer in Europe. And one might well have expected her to have been thoroughly spoiled by such an appreciation of critics and the devotion of the public.

But this was not the case. On the contrary, Karsavina remained, as she had always been, deeply absorbed in her art. The phrase as applied to her is true—it contains nothing of the specious or commonplace. She had devoted considerable study to the old productions in an ardent and passionate search for herself. She had found herself in the renaissance of the ballet, which brought her world-wide fame. But, whether in doubt of her strength or in an atmosphere of adulation, she had never ceased working; jealously conserving her powers and following the advice of critics for their improvement. She incessantly strove after perfection, and her progress in it had been steady. While her patient and assiduous toil remained the secret of the classroom, of the rehearsal and of the 'wings'; before the footlights she appeared to be ever growing in inspiration, in technique and also in the art of *mime*—her movements seemed to gain continually in facility, finish and elaboration.

It is of small concern to a spectator how an artist masters his art. One may attain his *apogée* all at once. Another may have to study stubbornly and unceasingly merely to achieve a little. It is only the result that is important, not the manner of its achievement. The artist accomplishes his or her aim whether the public realises the arrival of a new constellation or not. This growth of Karsavina's powers was evident on every occasion of her return home from her tours. Each time she was seen to be gaining in completeness. She reached the tenth anniversary of her *début* amid unfailing laudation and success. To her the date was of consequence since it marked the mid-stage of her career as an artist.

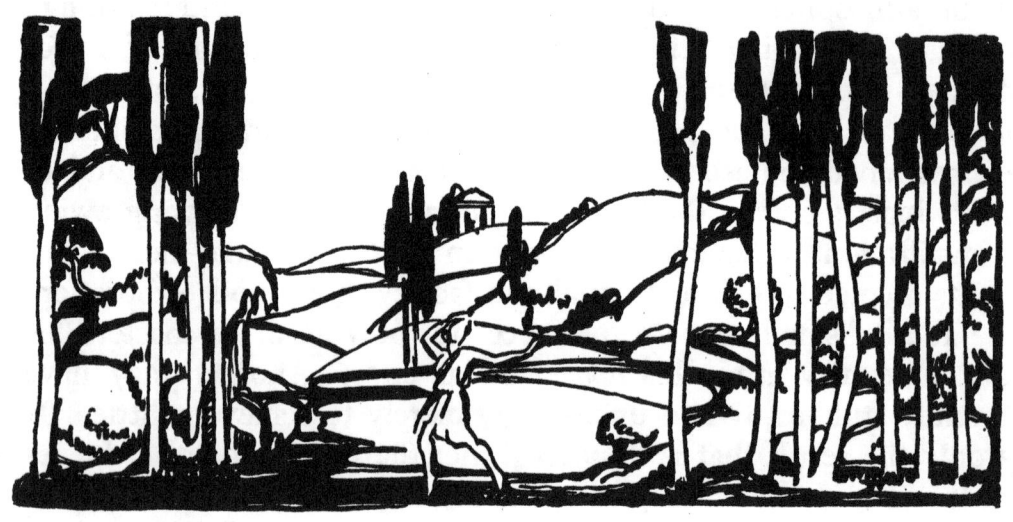

TEN YEARS

IN the course of the preceding chapters I have mentioned that the individuality, the personality of a *ballerina* is moulded during the early years of her ballet experience. It is then that her technique is formed. Talent may reveal itself at the earliest appearances of a little girl fresh from the dancing-school; but the improvement, the transition of these childish abilities into a power, takes time. It must proceed gradually. The public may see it developing, but the mystery of that development lies in the psychological depths of the artist's temperament.

We have now known Karsavina for ten years. For a considerable period before this anniversary the public, critics, painters and sculptors in Paris, St. Petersburg and London had acclaimed her as the leading dancer. Her *répertoire* included *rôles* of a diverse nature, a fact in itself sufficient to prove the rare versatility of her talent and the immense range of her choregraphic knowledge. Now versatility in art is a priceless possession. It infers the precious quality of self-dissatisfaction—of ever seeking new means of improvement and conquest. If I were asked to say whether I considered Karsavina an artist who has arrived at the zenith of her powers and whose limitations are reached, I should answer, with deep conviction, ' No ! ' . . . Karsavina is still *un monde en création*, though *rôles* of artistic value which belong definitely to the past may be found in her *répertoire*.

Thus : her nymph *Echo* in *Narcisse*, where, without dancing a step, Karsavina produces a tragic vision of antique beauty unforgettable in the history of the art of the ballet. The simplicity of the means employed to evoke the picture is remarkable. Scarcely a technical accessory is visible in her execution of the *rôle*. The entire effect is left to inner flame—to the spirit-glow of the semi-goddess whose tenderness has been mocked by the one she loves. Only by means of this mystic lamp are the depths of *Echo's* soul seen and understood.

In *Les Sylphides*, Karsavina glides in the moonlight through forest glades, among tall trees and undergrowth. Phantom companions surround her as she dances to the melancholy strains of the arch-dreamer Chopin. She is a sylph, an elemental spirit of the air. She has no more *rôle* than the ballet has literary object. She is of the kingdom of pure dancing, of dancing for dancing's sake. The choregraphic production clothes the music with plastic movement. By the seemingly simple mechanism of a dance, without ornament or virtuosity, a perfect image of the mysterious, ethereal female spirit is produced; a vision of the romantic period so often seen in creations of 1830, when the stage was invaded by elves, sylphs, dryads, goblins and other secondary mythical beings.

In *Le Spectre de la Rose* we have the same romanticism, transferred from the realm of fantasy to that of everyday life. Karsavina shows us the love-dream of a sentimental Victorian maid.

Again, in Schumann's *Carnaval*, she appears in the romantic manner of a time passionately struggling with middle-class philistinism, though the choregraphic character and mode of execution of the ballet are different.

For the sake of contrast, I have taken two totally different epochs—the ancient Greek and the romantic. Now let us behold her as *Armide*, the mysterious enchantress of the pompous times of Louis XIV. In this ballet, she moves in the brilliantly artificial environment of a French court, among Le Nôtre's curiously-clipped yews, arbours, pavilions, statues, fountains and cascades. It is the century of ceremonial, etiquette, gorgeous raiment, low bows and strange rumours. Again, Karsavina correctly interprets the style of the day. Her dancing expresses its character with truth and clearness.

Then we have another tale, this time a popular Russian one, as far removed from ancient Greece as from eighteenth-century France. Indeed, it has nothing in common with Western imagination of any period whatsoever. Karsavina, incarnate as the *Fire Bird*, once more awakes our wonder. Her fluttering steps, her frightened eyes, which remind us of those pictures painted by Vroubel, her bird-like tremors in brutal hands—evoke a picture full of Russian character. Curiously enough the Russian folk-lore tale has a savour of the East. The connection is still more noticeable when studying the affinity between Eastern and Slavo-Russian epics, though at first sight the Perso-Arabian orientalism of *Schéhérazade* has little in common with the Russian orientalism of *L'Oiseau de Feu*.

In Karsavina's list of plastic productions her Eastern *rôles* hold a preponderant place. The Sultana *Zobeide* in *Schéhérazade*, *Ta-hor* in *Une Nuit d'Egypte*, the Khan's wife in *Islamei*, *Thamar* in *Thamar*, are all creations of artistic merit. They are full of tone and colour. The indolent passions of the East, the sudden tragedies of the *harêm*, the close perfumes from which a woman's soul longs to escape into light and air, in revolt and protest against slavery; all is exquisitely expressed by Karsavina. She creates the sombre figure of *Queen Thamar* with an apparent minimum of effort. The union of two opposite longings of the human spirit, a burning and ever-unsatisfied thirst for love and death, is rendered with a fine tact which never oversteps the border between an artistic image and a clinical case.

It is far from my intention to enumerate all the ballets in Karsavina's extensive *répertoire*. In this chapter, which is devoted to a brief recapitulation of her first ten years' activity, I am taking only a few of her new ballet *rôles*. But I have no hesitation in saying that Karsavina occupies in the region of Fokine's productions (following that of Petipa), not only an important place, but the only one. No other dancer dances the whole of Fokine's *répertoire*. And as for the older ballets, those of Petipa, when in Russia, Karsavina appears in every one. She dances in *Raymonda*, in *La Belle au Bois Dormant*, in *Casse Noisette*, in *Le Lac des Cygnes*, in *Paquita*, in *Koniok Gorbounok*, in *Le Corsaire* and many others.

When speaking of the ballets of this period, it is well to remember that the critical method I have ventured to apply to the new ballet is useless in determining a *ballerina's* merits in the old. The reason is that style, type, epoch, the influence of such and such a period on certain phases of choregraphic production are there non-existent. In such ballets as *La Belle au Bois Dormant*, *Casse Noisette*, *Koniok Gorbounok*, it can be said, without fear of contradiction, that no real *rôle* (as such) exists for the leading dancer. *Aurore*, the *Fairy*, the *Girl King*, can be recognised only by reference to the programme, by the exceptional beauty of the costume or by the magnitude of the *rôle* in the ballet. . . . The leading dancer appeared and danced. She occupied a particular spot on the stage. She danced in a particular way, quite independently of the dramatic interest—supposing there to have been any—sometimes in direct disaccord with it. Even in ballets which contained dramatic interest, such as *Le Lac des Cygnes*, *Paquita*, and *Le Corsaire*, the means of expression employed by Petipa were scanty, primitive and uniformly the same. Now and then short pantomimic scenes were introduced, to be followed by dances having no sort of connection with them, nothing in the way of dramatic exposition or opportunity for plastic drama.

The old ballet must be taken for what it was, for its historical value, for its use as an academy of classical choregraphy. It must not be judged by the canons of the modern pantomimic drama. Certainly, dancing occupied the chief place in Petipa's ballets. The *ballerina* had to be a classical expert, and also highly proficient in technique. Karsavina began her studies in the old classical school. She received a strictly classical bringing-up in our ballet academy, and, having learned all it could teach her, she continued to study under various other professors. I have mentioned this already, and also that, at the outset of her career in 1903, she underwent a severe illness, from which she recovered slowly. The physical strength required by the virtuosities of classical dancing returned tardily, and for some considerable time there was a weakness in her performance which caused her to lack that brilliancy, that *brio*, on which dancers of great physical strength are apt to pride themselves.

Tricks of preciosity were for a long time the fashion on the Russian stage. They had been introduced by the Italians, especially by Legnani. The habit ended by bringing about an absurd spirit of acrobatic rivalry, which quickly developed into gross artistic exaggeration. Karsavina seemed to foresee the approaching decline of the classical cult. Her artistic taste rebelled at the spectacle of a dancer striving perpetually after acrobatic tricks in technique and a skill in the mechanical part of her art that might easily lead beyond the limits of truth.

Not only were many years of toil needed to encompass results of so doubtful a value, but the fragrance, beauty and poetry of dancing suffered in the process. They were unable to survive these intricacies of the gymnasium. Karsavina understood that a serious study of technique was indispensable as the basis of dancing, if only to free the artist's creative skill from too close an environment by matter, and she also understood that it is when technique passes unnoticed by the spectator, that the dancer may be considered to have mastered this underlying principle of her art. If well considered, this ceases to be paradoxical.

During the first ten years of her career Karsavina attained to a high rank as a classical performer. Her dancing was entirely free from vulgarity, well under control, classic in the strictest and fullest meaning of the word. She had an instinctive feeling for measure, an unfailing sense of the bounds beyond which love of pose becomes the mere rigidity of the equilibrist. An inartistic nature, carried away by an ambition to make records in virtuosity, naturally oversteps the artistic limits of classicism. Of this, Karsavina was well aware. She consciously avoided such tricks. They were not necessary to her. Her art already furnished a correct model of the truly classic dance, exquisite in its simplicity of thought and in the severe beauty of its form.

Karsavina's classical dancing is melodious with the unspoken poetry of gesture and pantomime, more eloquent than any words. Of late her art has acquired new qualities in this direction. It has become still more thoughtful and poetic, while her dancing has penetrated the secrets of a technique which, leaving mere effect on one side, is fully expressive of her appreciation of the beautiful. It has attained to the noble level of the French classicism which reigned supreme on the European stages and our own, until we were invaded by the later Italians, who drew it from its right path into the devious æsthetics of the circus.

Since we have not yet reached the later stages of Karsavina's career, a final conclusion as to her artistic activities must be left till later. I have spoken of her period of study, of her wanderings in the vast kingdom of Terpsichore. I have pointed out the flexibility and delicacy of her talent, and that she continued to be dissatisfied with achieved results in a limited sphere. I have shown her looking forward to new horizons—to new worlds. A dancer, who performs for an unlimited number of times in a few ballets of definite type, attains in them to a certain determinate perfection that to her may mean a very creditable tradition. But real talent is never satisfied with such attainment. It is too early for Karsavina to rest on her laurels.

THE HEIGHT

FROM her tours Karsavina has always returned to her national theatre with rejuvenated spirit. While perfecting her talents in the new *répertoire*, she has striven to apply its methods to the old classical school, so far as they could be made to embrace its huge choregraphic bulk. It had become apparent to every one that something different, something new, had found its way into her acting and dancing. Her former timidity and lack of self-confidence had disappeared. She danced with freedom, audacity and inspiration. She was entrusted with a *répertoire* immense in its range. It consisted of ballets of the ancient cycle prior to Tchaikovsky; those of Tchaikovsky; of Glazounoff; Fokine—from first to last—the *Préludes*, and *Islamei;* Romanoff's ballets, Drigo's, and a whole host of others.

It was the flexibility of talent she had acquired abroad that enabled her to face without fear so varied and extensive a *répertoire* —now as a classical dancer, perfect from a technical point of view; now as a dramatic artist in pantomime; now as a *mime* in scenes of lyric fantasy or comedy; and now as a performer of the new ballet, in which her great talent found the fullest expression. Once she has mastered the style of the production, she is able to bring out not only its salient, but its most esoteric, characteristics. Nor do the realms of mimetic drama or dancing hold any secrets from her.

At first, the young artist was regarded by the public with surprise, and with some reserve. People appeared sceptical and a little astonished at her very eclectic tastes. They were in doubt as to whether Karsavina really was an artist of unusual ability.

It is not easy to forget Karsavina's appearance in *Giselle*, and I propose to dwell a little upon this ballet. It contains a very responsible part for the *ballerina*. When she appeared in it the ballet was already old-fashioned; and, moreover, was very rarely staged owing to the difficulty of finding a suitable leading dancer. A. Pavlova had reintroduced it to our stage, and enjoyed in it an overwhelming reputation. People still remembered her for her success in *Giselle*. Therefore, it was somewhat presumptuous of a young artist to dare to appear where Pavlova, with her tragic acting, had already triumphed.

Giselle has certain unfading characteristics as a ballet. It is a ballet *par excellence* for a romantic artist with poetical delicacy of execution. It is pervaded by the tender and artless fancies of the 'thirties, which preserve it from oblivion. Karsavina's interpretation was centred in the fascination of the scenic image she evoked. It was simple, tender and beautiful. She offered an explanation of the difficult and conventional mad scene by her subtle rendering of the growth of the tragedy in the soul of the betrayed woman. She succeeded in blending together separate dramatic moments into one artistic whole. She gave a picture both harmonious and convincing.

The difficulty of the *rôle* lies in the suddenness with which the drama develops, but Karsavina's mastery of the part overcomes this. Her dramatisation of the character, even during the most violent crisis of insanity, always retained the delicate savour of lyrical romance. By some process of artistry peculiar to herself, she maintains this sentiment all through the second act, which is pure choreography.

Gently, sorrowfully, she weaves dances clouded by unsatisfied longings for past happiness, and in this plastic movement of a woman beyond earthly troubles she subtly preserves the connection between the visionary and the real. The dancer remembers the joys and griefs of the past, but the recollection brings no further misery to a freed soul.

The means for the expression of style are of prime importance in the representation of bygone epochs, and Karsavina's powers in that respect are remarkable. Consider the *adagio* in the second act; the brilliancy of the *variations* and *coda*. Her success in the *rôle* of *Giselle* was complete. She was able to remain herself, to lose nothing of her originality, to produce no copy of her famous predecessor nor to suggest any imitation. She had her own interpretation, in which she gave the character quite a new direction, fresh lines, colours and tonality. A. Pavlova had been passionate and tragic in the part. Karsavina's aim was to produce an elegy, a lyric. She translated a fairy tale into a drama of life, the symbolism of which she expressed in a sad and melancholy story.

The old ballet *Giselle* took on a new existence after being rehabilitated, first by A. Pavlova and then by Karsavina. In the modern *répertoire* it earned that right of place which it maintains. It is synthetic, concise and compact. It has no unnecessary details, and, without exaggeration, may be styled a 'primitive' of the romantic period. Its manner is full of relief, and its rhythm spiritual and lifelike. But the artist required for the title *rôle* must be capable of bringing out these qualities, capable of exhaling the perfume of olden times and restoring the beauty of faded colours. Karsavina, who is, above all, poetic, gave of her best to the classic dancing and highly dramatic scenes which the *rôle* afforded her.

Any one who had witnessed Karsavina's first steps, who had followed her self-searchings, who had watched with pleasure the growth of her talent and had encouraged her on her difficult and often unnoticed path to popularity, could hardly have been surprised at her success in an inspired production such as *Giselle*.

She was now to prove herself an equally inspired artist in Fokine's *Une Nuit d'Egypte*. It is interesting to compare these two ballets, which on one occasion happened to be given on the same night.

Giselle and *Une Nuit d'Egypte* are at the opposite poles of choregraphy. One is in the style of the old and charming romanticism of Gautier; the other—the last word of the new ballet! . . . Presented in quick succession, these two ballets, each typical of the epoch it represents, acquire new piquancy. They leave the sources of art far behind. Both treat of the same subject, that of a simple, trustful and loyal love. In both are depicted a young woman's broken heart, her betrayal, and the death of her lover.

Thamar Karsavina in Giselle, from the statue by Soudbinin

The difference lies in the total visual impression produced. *Giselle* presents a graceful picture, painted *à tempera*, without vividness. The feeling left is that of the romantic melancholy of a dream dreamed on a moonlight summer night. The psychology of the drama is not always expressed in suitable colours, and they are at all times conventional. The dances illustrating the drama are seldom justified by the situation—the whole action of the ballet is far from spontaneous. A delightful and truly human story makes it possible, and if its mechanism fails to shock, it is because it is an indispensable adjunct of the old manner.

Une Nuit d'Egypte, on the contrary, is the work of a new artist. Bright and vivid colours proclaim the joy of living. The psychology of the drama is well maintained and its plastic interpretation made to correspond with the situation as well as with the music. The dances arise naturally out of the action. As in every scenic production, there is a certain amount of conventionality, but it is no longer that of the old school.

In the Karsavina of the first act, there was no longer any inprecision of a timid pupil who has learnt by heart her difficult lesson and fears to forget it. The emotions visibly illuminating the course of the action are original. The psychology of the part has been grasped, and the artist interprets it in her own way. In the dances of the second act her strength increases. Their poetic melancholy is weakened in no way by an almost faultless technique. To the end the young dancer preserves intact the mystic style of the romantic tale. This fact is worth noting. To judge merely by the artist's earlier independent attempts at creation—and the faculty of personification is the dancer's most precious gift—one could hardly have expected Karsavina to become so soon a star of the first magnitude.

The Karsavina of *Une Nuit d'Egypte* is totally different from the Karsavina of *Giselle*. She plays the same tragedy of a betrayed girl's broken heart, but in a tone more realistic, more decided. She takes as firm a hold of the style of the production as she does in *Giselle*, but in a more dramatic manner. However, her performance of the part of *Ta-Hor* has been referred to already among Karsavina's foreign triumphs and need not be dwelt upon again here.

WHILE a review of Karsavina's entire *répertoire* is out of place, a few details may be useful concerning her more important creations, in order that no doubt may remain as to the scope of her talent. For this purpose it will be enough to refer to the cycle of St. Petersburg productions comprising the ballets of the old masters, St. Léon, Petipa, Ivanoff and others. They have been left to the world as legacies of the old classical school, creations on which its *répertoire* was based. They will probably be found on more modern programmes so long as the ballet is counted among State artistic institutions under a future Government of Russia.

La Bayadère is one of the most difficult of these ballets. It is a long, complicated production, consisting of pantomimic drama and many arduous dances. Karsavina's chief hindrance in *Bayadère*, however, lay not so much in the mastery of choreographic and mimetic details in the *rôle* of *Nikia* as in the fact that she followed a *ballerina* with a great and solid reputation in the part: one, moreover, much and justly admired by the public—A. Pavlova. . . .

Nevertheless, the public accorded Karsavina a warm welcome. They recognised at once that she gave her dancing and acting a correct tone: that while she presented a well-studied picture, her drama was expressive and full of colour. The actual dances need not be mentioned. As executed by Karsavina they were delicate, plastic, and graceful. They suited the dancer, since no other has so beautiful a *port de bras* (carriage of the arms). She never loses sight for a moment of the proper interconnection of her limbs. When preparing for a pirouette, a moment when she has to gather together all her strength, and when most dancers lose control over the necessary accord of arms and legs, she has complete command of her body. The *adagio* is always the best test of a dancer's classical abilities. During this slow movement she is in full evidence. No trick can conceal a false attitude, a hesitating movement, or the absence of musical ear or technique. Karsavina's *adagio* in the *Ghosts* of *La Bayadère* is remarkable for choregraphic self-control. In the classical *rôles* of the old ' dancing ' ballets she displays a nobility of manner, the very seal of severe classicism, a true sentiment of rhythm and a wonderfully faultless technique.

There is also much genuine acting in the dramatic portions of this ballet which obviously have been very carefully studied from the point of view of form. There is artistic gradation and climax in the psychologic action. Lastly, there is a general conception, a sentiment of measure and style, and an exquisite scenic image full of lyricism, womanly charm and plastic grace. Karsavina gives new life and youth to the old ballet. She brings to the *rôle* of *Nikia* a warm and genuine note, besides importing into her dancing all the poetry of the East.

As *Medora*, Karsavina has revived another moribund ballet. *Le Corsaire* is a dull production, based on Byron's famous poem. Its music is quite insignificant, and only a very talented artist can make the ballet presentable. While drawing a bewitching picture of the young Greek girl, Karsavina distributes throughout the ballet the drama and mimetic expression now universally identified with her name.

The distinguishing features of her dancing are the absence of all exaggeration, the toning down of conventionality; briefly, dramatic tact. The grotto scene which, owing to its bad composition, might easily be made to appear ridiculous, is saved by her *savoir faire*. The same may be said of such trifles as *Finesse d'amours*, the *Little Corsair*, and others like them, which become delicate miniatures, finely and tastefully executed. She gives a totally different complexion to the *Little Corsair*, transforming it into a work of art full of originality and distinction. She converts a commonplace dance, formerly considered so unnecessary an episode as to be sometimes omitted, into a charming and interesting interlude.

In doing this she relies on nothing cheap or doubtful in the manner of effect. The *Little Corsair* is, of course, a wholly negligible affair, but Karsavina's execution of it transforms it into a fascinating bagatelle. And throughout each of these last-mentioned *rôles*, whatever their innate importance, her classical manner never fails to be elegant to the point of severity. She neither strives after easy laurels nor employs inartistic devices. While becoming a great artist, she has found that there is in dancing a limit of true classicism, and this she never oversteps. This kind of dancing was not intended to achieve vulgar, flashy effects, but to satisfy the requirements of recognised connoisseurs. To say this is to explain why Karsavina's dancing is appreciated by those of advanced discernment in the art.

A very choice classicism is exhibited by her in the *pas de deux* in the third act of *Le Jardin Animé* (music by L. Delibes). Here, also, her classical dancing is brilliant—gay, lively, with a remarkable sentiment of rhythm, an accomplished technique and great beauty of line.

In truth, it is not going too far to say that there is youth, freshness and charm in all her dancing. Everything in it is elegant, simple and noble.

A third old-fashioned ballet, *Don Quichotte*, entirely revised and produced on the St. Petersburg stage by the Moscow *maître-de-ballet*, A. Gorsky, afforded Karsavina another opportunity for the display of her exceptional ability. *Don Quichotte* demands a specifically ethnographic colouring. The *maîtres-de-ballet* before Gorsky did not pay much attention to national style in dancing, or to ethnographic peculiarities in the characters represented. In such cases they contented themselves with a distant and scarcely more than suggested similarity, to which end they introduced into their choreography a sprinkling of popular conventional details designed to denote a national character in the production.

Naturally, nothing artistic could be made of such a tradition, for the dancing slavishly followed the musical score, even when this was totally devoid of any kind of specially national savour; though, to produce ethnographic colour, it should be deeply impregnated with this.

The lovely Spanish picture Karsavina presented was beautifully expressed in the passionate Iberianism of her dancing. Her execution includes several complicated and daring *pirouettes*, brilliant *entrechats* and precise *pointes*.

In a previous chapter I have taken the opportunity to explain why the test of a classical dancer lies in the slow movement of the *adagio*—where defects of execution are especially difficult to conceal. This is the test which Karsavina triumphantly passes. Her dancing in the *variation* to the *Dreams* beginning with repeated and brilliant *entrechats* and ending with *jetés en tournant*, is exceedingly effective. Equally successful are her *fouettés en diagonale* in the last tableau.

A still older Spanish ballet on the St. Petersburg stage is *Paquita*. It has remained in the *répertoire* untouched and unaltered since its composition, perhaps fortunately so, because it has preserved its air of an ancient lithograph, very much faded, but which has kept—as a beautiful remembrance—the subtle perfume of a withered, treasured flower.

The *rôle* of *Paquita* consists of simple, unpretentious drama ; again in the manner of the old romantic ballet, with its many conventional and ingenuously primitive situations. But if we take into account the far-off date of the ballet's composition, it is still remarkably effective and presentable on the stage. Karsavina's pantomime and her knowledge of style are so consummate that the want of spontaneity of the old production vanishes immediately. The picture created is of an indefinable quality. It is both deliciously youthful and nobly plastic.

In the long dramatic scene of the second act, the dancer's miming reaches to such a height of power and enthusiasm as to dominate the spectator. Ample relief is afforded to the *rôle's* dramatic side without detracting from its vividness of expression. Throughout the whole of the second act, which is really one continued and arduous scene of dumb show, Karsavina dances not only with vivacity, but also with a complete understanding of the demands of plastic line and curve. The choreographic part of the *rôle* is taken with great brilliancy and charm, also with regard for form, while her technique is imbued with the tender spell of a pensive romanticism. Altogether a fine chiselling of details, a rich variety of pose and an elegant finish in the outline and quality of the dance ! . . . A whole academy of *attitudes, pirouettes, pointes* and other technical details are included in this difficult *adagio*.

The dancer makes a few alterations (pretty and graceful *emboités*) at the end of the *variation*, which improve its effectiveness and make it correspond more entirely with the rhythm of the music. The classical dances are given a Spanish atmosphere by means of certain slight curves of the body, by a particular contour and movement of the arms, and by an occasional arresting, inclined pose of the figure—finely expressed, and neither abrupt nor too accentuated. It is altogether a remarkable performance.

The old ballet *répertoire* contains very few strictly Russian ballets. Among these are *Le Poisson d'Or*, long since forgotten and not now produced, and *Le Petit Cheval Bossu*. The latter has run through an immense number of performances and is still given, though renovated and somewhat altered in form by Gorsky.

Concerning the pantomime of the *rôle* of the *Girl King*, little is to be said. The drama is inexpressive and, from the *mime's* point of view, the artist has little to do. There remain to be considered the scenic images created and the dancing. Out of elements of fairy-like fancy, Karsavina produces a bewitching princess. The picture is full of fantasy and colour, the plasticity beyond criticism. The same may be said of the *rôle's* choreography—whether in Drigo's purely classical *variation* in *Nereids*, in the semi-classical dance on *pointes*, or in the conventionally national style of Tchaikovsky's Russian dance. In these, Karsavina's technique is never conspicuous, never obvious. She never accentuates it in difficult places. She makes no call on the attention of connoisseurs to witness its perfection—by that very fact raising it to a high artistic level. Indeed her technique, as such, is quite unobtrusive. It is only one element among many out of which a gifted artist-dancer creates a highly perfected style.

As Karsavina takes it, the part becomes one of much choreographic brilliancy. It would be difficult to go further in the sense of the picturesque in this kind of dancing. The dancer achieves a perfection of line and a very deft chiselling of separate details. All this is the natural outcome of a great capacity which focusses and exacts attention, becomes the centre around which all interest revolves; so that in admiring it, the onlooker forgets the dullness of a long libretto, the defects of an antiquated *mise en scène*, a cumbersome *corps de ballet*, and too many solo dances.

Karsavina made her *début* as leading dancer in the *Petit Cheval Bossu*. Manifestly her dancing then cannot be compared with her

dancing since her triumphs abroad. Her periodical returns to the stage of the *Mariynsky Theatre* have enabled her to rejuvenate many old productions and to keep alive the public's interest in them.

THE Tchaikovsky ballets may be next considered. Although of later composition than those just mentioned, these belong rather to the ancient *répertoire* than to the new. Their modernism lies in their music, which leaves far behind the primitive scores of *Le Petit Cheval Bossu* and *Le Corsaire*.

Each is a symphony in rich and varied form and with a skilfully worked out orchestration. But the subject-matter is insignificant. It is invariably a fairy tale without dramatic incident. Tchaikovsky, who had written many dramatic operas, appeared to have avoided drama intentionally in his ballets. He gave them an exclusive choregraphic and symphonic shape. Of his three, only the *Lac des Cygnes* has a dramatic situation, and this is but crudely outlined. In *La Belle au Bois Dormant* and *Casse Noisette* there are no mimetic scenes whatever, unless the scene with the spinning wheel in the former is counted as such, and in any case *La Belle au Bois Dormant* cannot be dramatised owing to its excessive shortness. On the other hand, the choregraphic composition of the Tchaikovsky ballets differs scarcely at all from those of the older *répertoire*. There is the same number of separate *variations, pas de deux, pas d'action, adagios, ensembles*, waltzes, and scenes of comedy. The entire choregraphic material bears the character of a big *divertissement* unrelated to the action. This fact is explicable by his having worked with Petipa, who was unable to conceive of a ballet as a drama, as did Fokine, Romanoff, and others of the modern school. To him it was purely a dancing affair; the more so, perhaps, since his creative work was on the decline, and his dramatic situations—simply planned and without relation to the dancing—no longer satisfied the demands of the public.

In *Le Lac des Cygnes* there is a certain amount of dramatic action. The double *rôle* of *Odetta-Odilia* was composed for two dancers, and formerly was interpreted in that way. Except in likeness, the tender, romantic *Odetta*, wandering in fairy visions, has no resemblance to *Odilia*, the crafty daughter of the evil genie; and this fact might have led to drama, but does not do so. Both the *grand pas des cygnes* of *Odetta*, and the *pas d'action* of *Odilia* are in the same manner of traditional classicism, and have little bearing on the character of the ballet as a dramatic composition. It would take a highly gifted dancer, accomplished in pantomime, to give the public any clear idea of the two personages.

However, Karsavina is such a dancer. Her understanding is exact of measure and of the bounds beyond which lie inartistic acrobatic exercises and this despite the fact that the present increasing admiration for technical virtuosity makes the æsthetic limits of classicism difficult to define. Karsavina possesses this power in a high degree, and in this lies her strength as a classical dancer. As regards the drama in *Le Lac des Cygnes*, I must confess to a preference for her romanticism among the mysterious ruins, to the demoniacal character she assumes at the festival in the castle. The one develops a lyrical story in a natural manner; the other is marred by the pensive tenderness of her picture, which does not answer to the idea of an evil spirit possessing the magician Rotbart's daughter.

In the second tableau of the first act the dancer's *adagio* is a remarkable example of severe classical style. Her dances in the last *tableau* also leave a fine impression. But the choregraphic conception of *Odetta-Odilia* is difficult for a single dancer to realise. It is not easy to concentrate two distinct and different types in one person. The attempt necessarily results in want of unity in the plastic exposition of the *rôle*. Yet Karsavina satisfactorily performs the impossible. In certain portions of the part, especially in the *variation* in which Pierrina Legnani used to gain such unbounded applause by her thirty-two equilibrist *fouettés*, Karsavina overcomes all difficulties. The period of enthusiasm for exaggerated Italian virtuosity has long passed, and Karsavina executes the *variation* as an artist of taste and æsthetic comprehension, excluding from it all inartistic display of technical skill not justified by the demands of the music or the dancing. She gives the last act quite the character of an elegy. Legnani had not attained to so exalted an ideal of poetic charm.

La Belle au Bois Dormant is, as I have said, a purely dancing ballet. Nothing need be said of it in any other sense. Composer and *maître-de-ballet* have contrived in it a big choreographic display for the leading dancer, and have given it the character of a long concerted *divertissement*. In these circumstances the *rôle* of *Aurore* could not be of much interest to Karsavina, whose talent lies rather in the direction of drama. The part brought forward one side only of her artistic individuality, the choreographic.

Of late, Karsavina's dancing has aroused, by its technical brilliancy, an ever-increasing interest. Refinement and spirituality appear more and more in her classicism. From the flower of her talent has come brilliancy of form and colour. Even in so essentially technical a *rôle* as *Aurore*, composed exclusively for the leading dancer to display a complicated classicism, Karsavina evinces lyric poetry in her performance. She creates a verse of plastic song.

An amusing 'critical' article may be mentioned here. It was dedicated to Karsavina in the part of *Aurore*. The critic speaks of an 'erotic arabesque' and of her 'trembling legs.' It is possible, of course, to arrive at so extraordinary a conclusion, if dancing is to be looked at from so extraordinary a point of view. Karsavina's dancing is characterised by its complete chastity, by its want of suggestion, and its perfect simplicity. But what precisely does 'erotic arabesque' mean, and how is it possible for a dancer to have trembling legs? If her legs trembled, she certainly could not dance.

What is really remarkable about *La Belle au Bois Dormant*, apart from the grace and charm of the execution, is the manner in which an artistic feeling of measure has displaced the intricate equilibrium of the Italian school.

The choreographic interest of *Aurore* consists in three appearances of the *ballerina*; in a *grand pas d'action* with the suitors, the shade of *Aurore*; and the *pas de quatre* of *Aurore*, *Desireé* and two *Fairies*. In these, Karsavina is a dancer of classical technique having all the required virtuosity. She possesses the amazing qualities of being as interesting in the old style as in the new. In *Aurore* she was the successor of *ballerinas* of great technical ability. And she differs from those predecessors by the 'eternal feminine' in her which adds delicate colour to her classicism. Her execution is perfectly finished in pose and plasticity. The suppleness and softness of her body, together with her unapproachable *port de bras*, convey an impression of dancing expressed by sculpture. As a picture, as a scenic vision, she is the loveliest of all Sleeping Beauties.

In the ballet *Casse Noisette*, the leading dancer appears only in the last act ; in a *pas de deux* in the manner of the old classical choreography. In this difficult measure Karsavina rises to the sublime. She is the *Fée Dragée* ; she evokes a fairy tale, a magic Christmas story. Her *adagio* is a plastic thought, exquisite as a song. She has surpassed in *Casse Noisette* all her predecessors : Legnani, Kshesinskaïa, Preobrajenskaïa—all great plastic artists, but not one of them, in this essentially choreographic *rôle* from the old classical *répertoire*, the equal of Karsavina.

LIKE Tchaikovsky, Glazounoff has also composed three ballets : *Les Saisons*, *Ruses d'Amour*, and *Raymonda*.

The first of these is composed of four allegorical *tableaux*, but contains no part for the leading dancer. In one of these *tableaux* Karsavina was allotted a brief choregraphic episode, the *Rose*, transparent as a water colour.

In *Ruses d'Amour*, which is founded on Watteau's paintings, Karsavina as the young countess, *Isabella*, revives classic French dancing with a certainty and elegance which amply recall the period. The simple outlines, for instance, the epoch of Camargo, again necessitate a choreography which remind the spectator of water colour. And the lovely music of A. K. Glazounoff greatly heightens the effect. Karsavina's *Isabella*, seen in the highly decorative garden, among exceedingly well-mannered companions, is playful and coquettish. Her fantasy is delightful, and she introduces that measure which always increases the value of creative work. During the latter half of her artistic career she has been particularly enamoured of the courtly French dances of the eighteenth century.

Raymonda is Glazounoff's longest ballet. It includes two pantomimic scenes; the first, *Raymonda's* dream of a Saracen soldier whose embrace she escapes; the second, her fear for her lover's life, in the duel scene. She interprets both with much expression. Her dramatic powers, however, have no great opportunity for display. The ballet, unlike *Giselle*, is not a drama of emotion common to all humanity. But, from the standpoint of dancing, she is irreproachable. Her performance was particularly appreciated by those versed in the finesse and intricacy of classical dancing. She was more especially noticed in the first *tableau* of the first act; while in the *pas classique hongrois* of the last act her *variations* were surprising.

To continue the review of the great dancer's performances more or less in order, we may briefly refer to such ballets as *Les Caprices du Papillon*, *The Fairy of the Dolls*, *Arlequinade*, and *La Fille Mal Gardée*. The poetical butterfly, whose caprice torments the enamoured grasshopper, is very originally danced. With Karsavina, trivial purpose and small technical detail disappear, and in her interpretation of the *rôle* we see less of conventional ballet routine than of a tender lyricism and love of the spring. Indeed, the atmosphere of springtime which pervades the ballet renders Karsavina's butterfly both artistic and natural. No less poetic is the fairy, who with a wave of her wand gives life to the dolls. While the coquettishly fascinating *Columbine* in the lengthy *Chasse aux Alouettes* is another example of conscientious classical dancing. There may be other colours, a different tone, a different design, but there is the same sincerity of execution without the unnecessary exaggerations and inartistic accentuations which are customarily so specially devised for the public's benefit. It was as *Columbine* that

Karsavina also appeared in Romanoff's charming work *Pierrot's Dream*. It is a small affair in the manner of a harlequinade. It contains three dramatic motives: *The Return from the Carnival*, *The Dream*, and *The Awakening*. Karsavina has already been styled the Queen of Columbines. In her performance of *rôles* like that of *Pierrot's Dream* she evokes the feeling of a pastoral of romantic lyricism. Her execution corresponds to Assaxieff's interesting and original music. Lastly, there is the capricious *Lise*, with her ingenuously child-like air, who succeeds in deceiving her aunt and in marrying *Colin*. The *ballerina* is charming in her fright at the cottage and in her tender passages with her lover. She gives the part a sense of comedy which carries away the spectator and arouses his merriment. It was in this ballet that the public were introduced to Karsavina's sense of comedy.

INCLUDED in the *répertoire* of the *Mariynsky Theatre* were many of Fokine's ballets. These were those he produced for Diaghileff abroad—*Les Sylphides, Une Nuit d'Egypte, Papillons, Le Pavillon d'Armide*; as well as others never performed out of Russia, for example, *Eunice, Islamei*, and *Les Preludes*.

The first four of these have been fully dealt with in the course of this book, and only a few further details need be given concerning Karsavina's performances in Fokine's St. Petersburg series. *Eunice* was his earliest ballet, and was composed after the manner of Isadora Duncan, in the plastic style of paintings on Greek vases.

Its method is that of the primitive, barefooted processional dance, which contained no *entrechats* and no *fouettés*, but which had in it beauty and a worship of the human form. In spite of its natural inequalities as a connecting link between the old school and the new, the first performance of *Eunice* produced a feeling of astonishment. Karsavina, with her beauty of ancient movement, her fine talent, the tender poetry of her dancing, and her natural grace, seemed to have been specially created to interpret the *rôle*.

Le Pavillon d'Armide, *Les Sylphides* and *Eunice* were given occasionally on the same evening. It was interesting to watch Karsavina transform herself from the gorgeous, mysteriously brilliant *Armide* into the sad and romantic *Sylphide*, and from that into the lovely *Eunice*. Such metamorphoses are possible only to an artist of infinite adaptability.

Papillons is a continuation of the famous *Carnaval*. The subject bears the choreographic stamp of a romantic century. The ballet, in the sense that it is a romantic blending of fancy and real life, harmonises perfectly with Schumann's music. The story is simple. Towards the end of the Carnival, girls arrayed in butterfly fancy dresses mystify a lonely *Pierrot*. There are a few charming scenes, *pas de deux*—*Pierrot* and the butterflies, the death and burial of a butterfly, her coming to life again, and a wedding dance. But the joyousness of carnival dies away; the fantastic dreams of the night vanish in the light of morning. The whole is conceived in a romanticism which harmonises exactly with the spirit of the music. Indeed, it is Schumann's music set in choreography and orchestrated by Tcherepnine. The story is merely *Pierrot's* dream of his mystification by a few joyous girls during the freedom of Carnival. Then the lights are extinguished. The revelry and noise die away. The pale dawn awakes and the gay fancies disappear with the darkness. Old folk and servants chaperon the girls home.

As a charming composition it might well be a sequel to Schumann's brilliant conception; as produced by Fokine—but it is best to consider it as an independent piece, for it has no connection with its great prototype *Carnaval*. As a repetition of style and of some of the situations the shorter piece lacks originality. It is only a variation on a well-worn theme.

Karsavina revels in the gaiety, the artistic simplicity and ingenuous sincerity of both productions. She understands the spirit of them, which she masters as an artist who loves the period. There is as much melody in her execution of the piece as there is in the music.

The story of the ballet *Islamei* is not unlike that of *Schéhérazade*. The heirs of Rimsky-Korsakoff—composer of the latter—protested against *Schéhérazade* being transformed into a choreographic work; while those of Balakireff, who wrote *Islamei*, objected to his music being used for a ballet. They consented only after long delay. *Islamei* was composed in 1869 on the theme of an Eastern *khorovod* which Balakireff had heard in the Caucasus. Since it was originally composed for the piano, S. M. Liapounoff orchestrated it. The score is melodious and well interprets the composition. The themes of both *Schéhérazade* and *Islamei* are, of course, taken from *The Thousand and One Nights*. In *Islamei* the subject-matter is simple and synthetically concise. It is the not uncommon story of a deceived husband. The favourite wife of the King of the Black Islands and Black Mountains gives her husband a sleeping draught in order that she may abandon herself to a negro. The King does not take the draught and makes pretence of sleeping. He witnesses the betrayal. The situation is practically identical with that in *Schéhérazade*. The King kills the negro, and the wife throws herself from a window into an abyss. The ballet throughout is Eastern in character and feeling, and is interrupted by only one brief dramatic scene and an *adagio*. It is nothing more than a variation and shorter edition of *Schéhérazade*, by which the *maître-de-ballet* was obviously inspired. It is related to *Schéhérazade* both in plot and tragic ending, as well as in the orgiastic nature of the dances. Anisfeld's decorations for it are beautiful, but it is inferior to *Schéhérazade* in brilliancy and in splendour. It is a highly concentrated drama of no great importance.

In the kaleidoscope of dances stage-managed by Fokine, the varying temper of the *harêm* and the oriental character of the dances are maintained in direct accord with the music. Outlined against such a background, Karsavina resembles an ancient Persian miniature. Her short scene of pantomime in *Islamei* is of the essence of a sensuous drama of the Eastern woman.

Les Preludes is one of Fokine's most original works. At the first performance public opinion was divided. Liszt's famous symphonic poem was written on Lamartine's *Poetical Meditations*.

The composer was inspired by the poet's philosophy—Life is a series of preludes to an unknown song, the first and anxious note of which is sung by Death.

To find a subject here for a ballet is not easy. Fokine succeeded by blending Liszt's melody with his own principles of plastic art. Lamartine's idea, a purely abstract one, was embodied in melody and rhythm, and Fokine's aim was to give these poetic and musical symbols a comprehensively plastic setting. His choregraphy corresponds very happily with Liszt's music and creates a concrete symbolism for Lamartine's thought. The result was a charming picture of light Botticelli figures, interlaced *en ronde* and silhouetted against the background of an old Italian picture. Karsavina is the central figure of the ballet. Her dancing is youthful, and is without the stiffness into which it might easily have drifted. She is the embodiment of a Botticelli painting.

A few unimportant parts in Karsavina's long and varied *répertoire* may have been omitted from the foregoing review. Every artist has some *rôles* which neither add to nor detract from his prestige. They need not change a note in the general aspect of the remarkable actress and dancer whose career has been given in these pages.

Of Karsavina's appearances on private stages or at charity performances little need be said. She possesses a considerable *répertoire* of concert dances and she appears at artists' and writers' clubs and associations. Of such artistic *cabarets* the *Wandering Dog* and the *Comedians' Rest* frequently welcomed her. A whole chapter might be devoted to so-called concert dances, for example, *Le Cygne*, of Saint-Saens ; also many dances of the eighteenth century arranged to contemporary music. In these she displays the same characteristics as in all her work : a subtle lyricism, a tendency to elegy in plastic movement, and a remarkable understanding of the style of an epoch.

CONCLUSIONS

TO all artists in the drama, and particularly to those in plastic form, physical appearance is important. In the long annals of dancing there are many who did not possess the gift of beauty, yet who, owing to their remarkable talents, left their names indelibly engraved on the page of history. Pierrina Legnani, the greatest *virtuosi* in technical dancing during the nineteenth century, was one of these. At an earlier epoch still, the famous Maria Taglioni was more remarkable for her art than for her beauty. The flattering lithographs and etchings which have come down from her time have sought to beautify their idol, but have been scarcely able to persuade this generation as to her good looks. Still, in an art which specially cultivates harmony of line and form, a good appearance is valuable. Karsavina has the gift by right of nature. She has no need of those artifices to which others, not so favoured, must resort. But it is only by seeing an artist on the stage that one may obtain a complete image. For only then does the inner meaning of the portrait appear and gain vitality through creative work.

Karsavina's face . . . pale, framed in an abundance of black hair . . . dark, thoughtful eyes, with sadness buried in their depths . . .

NOT only is formal physical beauty of importance to the dancer, but also the beauty of plastic movement. It is the foundation of every material form of choregraphy. The proportions of the different parts of the body one to the other, when set in motion, produce a reciprocity of line and form in space similar to that which rhythm produces in music. Dancing creates inevitably an idea of music, and is, therefore, musical; while, being also plastic, it is brought under the laws of proportion and rhythm. Dancing is related to sculpture. Both produce beauty of form. Dancing, following the rhythm of melody, renders musical emotion concrete. It materialises music. It transforms its sounds, as it does sculpture's contours, into plastic movement.

If sculpture is the statics of music, dancing is the dynamics of sculpture. . . .

Fokine showed in his ballets that to each musical note, even to every harmonic tone, there is a corresponding plastic movement. Plastic co-ordination is a most important element in plastic art, and it is one in which Karsavina excels. Nothing is less artistic than a dancer who, following the rhythm of the music, leaves her legs out of accord with her arms and her body out of accord with her head. In the ancient schools of choregraphy attention was almost exclusively given to the legs and the feet. A *figurante* of the old school was capable of performing prodigies of equilibrium with her feet without paying the slightest heed to the symmetry of pose of other parts of her body. The general effect and form of the dance were, of course, altogether lost. Flagrant examples of these and similar defects were manifested by many who imitated Legnani's celebrated step. While the legs were victoriously performing the thirty-two *fouettés*, the hands were waving about as independent and quite useless appendices. The head, which gave the impression of not being screwed on straight, swayed awkwardly from side to side, and the tired body drew the *figurante* aimlessly to different parts of the stage. Instead of being a brilliant trick, such as Legnani made it, the result was merely a contradiction to all plastic æsthetics.

The harmony of dancing is the due relation of simple and separate steps. Its melody is their link; their *enchaînement* is determinate rhythm. As a false note jars on the ear, so a false movement shocks the eye. In Karsavina's present dancing such crudities are absent. The plastic lines of her movements and attitudes have been perfected. Everything is in accord and harmony. Her *port de bras* is unfailingly correct, her body supple, the poise of her head all that it should be. Her legs are what the French call *intelligent*. No other word expresses the meaning so well. When the whole of this plastic organism is set in motion obeying the commands of melody and rhythm, the separate parts of the structure work in correspondence with each other in duly co-ordinated movements, and the result is the harmony and melody of the dance.

Though there is nothing now in Karsavina's dancing that looks forced, at the beginning of her career she failed in that softness and roundness of movement which later became its chief characteristic. At first there was angularity in the arms, a certain stiffness of the body. The legs had not completely mastered the dance's design—there were other imperfections. Happily the artist possessed discernment and the courage to realise her shortcomings and to work hard to eradicate them. Now, it can be said that she has succeeded. At the present moment no dancer understands better the plastics of classical dancing.

WHEN the *ballet-divertissement* gave place to the pantomimic-drama and the dancer's face was, for the first time, expected to express more than the eternal and stereotyped smile sanctified by tradition, mimetic expression became a first necessity for the *ballerina*. Since the development into new channels of the ballet *répertoire*, dramatic miming and technical virtuosity have become the essential accomplishments of the great dancer. An earlier stage of the growth of mimetic art can be referred back to the time when actors were first invited to remove their masks and women permitted on the stage in place of male counterfeits. This was in 1684, when Molli's ballet, *Le Triomphe de l'Amour*, marked the dawn of the pantomime ballet as now known. But still much remained to be done. Heavy, cumbersome costumes and enormous head-dresses still obscured the features, and a gradual deliverance from these was required to set free the dancer's body and leave visible her facial expression.

A general simplification of costume gave even the writers of ballets a wider scope. They were enabled to bring them out of the sphere of court etiquette into the domain of poetic fancy and realistic action.

Reformers persevered. Camargo (1710—1770) inaugurated comparatively short dresses while still preserving paniers. Clairon discarded paniers. Sallé adopted the Grecian tunic, but the famous Guimard (1762—1788) was the first to dress according to her *rôle* and to lay thereby the foundation of realism.

While the costume altered, giving greater freedom to the limbs, technique also underwent change. Dancing was more and more being allowed to interpret the theme, while dumb show gave ever clearer expression to pantomime. Only the subject-matter as yet failed to vary. It remained imprisoned in the iron circle of ancient myths. . . .

It was in a ballet of the period of Didelot that St. Leon and Petipa definitely introduced pantomime. It still lacked connection, it is true, with the ballet's choregraphic and musical elements. Still, whole dramatic scenes were introduced, as in the case of the first act of *Giselle*, or in the cabin scene of *La Fille du Pharaon*, or else in humorous scenes, as in *La Fille Mal Gardée*.

There remained many conventions and traditions, both of gesture and expression, but a great advance towards mimetic acting,

as compared with school tradition, came with Virginia Zucchi, an important figure in the realm of pantomimic drama. Anna Pavlova was a still greater innovator in this direction. It was she who created the images of *Giselle* and *La Bayadère*. Kshesinskaïa, in *Esmeralda* and *Fenella*, may also be mentioned ; and lastly, the dancer who is the subject of this book—Karsavina. . . .

Even in her case no one, during the first half of her career, could have prophesied her development into a remarkably gifted actress. This was achieved only by diligent study in an art freed from convention and prejudice. In the large picture gallery of Karsavina's creations there is a complete museum of mimetic expression. It includes a maiden's betrayed love (*Une Nuit d'Egypte*, *Giselle*) ; the sadness of the *Sylphide ;* the caprices of a poetical butterfly (*Papillons*) ; a cunning village hussy (*La Fille Mal Gardée*) ; playfulness and coquetry (*Le Carnaval*, *Arlequinade*, and other Columbines) ; romance of moonlit nights (*Le Spectre de la Rose*) ; deceptions of the *harêm* (*Schéhérazade*, *Islamei*) ; unrequited affection (*Narcisse*), besides many other moods and feelings, thoughts and pictures. Scarcely a situation can be imagined to which she has not contributed her interpretation.

Giselle and *Echo* are more generally accepted as the highest efforts of her genius in pantomime drama, though the comparative method, either as between work or people, is scarcely trustworthy in these cases. All true artists on the stage create their images in their own workshop by their own talents. They endow them with their own individuality of understanding, and there is little value in that comparison which involuntarily springs to the mind whenever a new work is presented.

The first creation of *Giselle* by C. Grisi cannot be judged. But A. Pavlova's interpretation of the *rôle* is still alive. She gave the tragedy of a woman's heart. She produced a powerful impression in the mad scene, and a fascinating one of sorrow in that of the *Willis*. It was a sombre tragedy, and her unforgettable picture of *Giselle* was the last cry of the tortured girl's spirit.

Karsavina took the part in another key. In her interpretation there enters no deep tragedy. On the contrary, it is a lyrical song of a woman's grief, sad and poetic. The pathos is tender, restrained. In the mad scene it is an almost timid complaint. In the act of the *Willis*, in all her dances, there is something soothing, almost a quiet satisfaction, a submission to fate and a hope for a happier future.

The *Giselle* of A. Pavlova tends to lacerate the nerves; that of Karsavina is eloquent and touching.

From the point of view of artistic value, and apart from the mood of the spectator, both questions as to which is the more truthful of these interpretations always will remain an insoluble problem. . . .

The nymph *Echo* has been frequently mentioned. Karsavina was the first to take this *rôle*. The absence of dramatic action and movement makes the part difficult. It proceeds almost entirely on spiritual considerations of suppressed feeling and disappointment. *Echo* loves *Narcissus*, who is unable to respond to a purely contemplative affection. *Echo's* longing—sorrowful, submissive, miserable—turns to a desire for death. The *rôle* consists of this. It is an arduous part to maintain. There is not one vivid scene, no colouring in details, no lines strongly drawn, only a silent longing of the soul—an intense grief.

Nevertheless, Karsavina's picture of the nymph moves the spectator deeply. So subtle a variety of shade, such delicacy in minutiæ, such perfect outline, with such beautiful and tender colour, interests him in this marvel of human life so intimately interwoven with this myth of far antiquity. Karsavina creates an ever-increasing, overwhelming sorrow, understood by the Greeks as Fate, Destiny—against which poignant despair, prayerful entreaty, bitter tears, are of no avail. Fate is Fate, and neither gestures nor appeal can avert it. And as grief distorts the human face—and the Hellenes were, before aught else, æsthetic—their natural resource was to throw a veil over the face, to exclude the glances of the curious. Karsavina, without actually concealing her features, gives a fine rendering of this sorrow and of its Hellenic atmosphere. It is not easy to describe in definite terms the means she employs. She has no specifically technical method, no particular movement of the eyes, eyebrows, lips; no gesture of the shoulders, arms or head. On the contrary, she economises gesture. Her method defies analysis. Perhaps it is less physical than spiritual. There appears to be something telepathic rather than visual in the way her inner emotions are conveyed to the audience, communicating to it her whole mood.

THE *ballerina* of to-day has a musical ear, and possesses a sense of rhythm as the soul of her craft. Being one of the poetic arts, dancing is closely allied to music. It for ever seeks rhythm, proceeds from it and creates it. Karsavina is both musical and rhythmical in her dancing. Rhythm withholds no secrets from her. She translates the most difficult modern music—*Islamei* and *Les Preludes*, for instance—into a choreography equally complicated and composed of sound and movement. But if rhythm is the aim of dancing, technique is the means of attaining it. And to acquire a brilliant technique demands years of tireless effort.

The technique of ballet-dancing, as now known, grew very gradually. Of simple beginnings, it was limited in the eighteenth century to the acquisition of certain definite things: a solemn, serious manner of walking, a few very primitive and simple steps, elegant bows and curtsies—in a word, *tenue*, deportment. It depended mainly on costume, as I have shown.

With the beginning of reform in that direction the technique of theatrical dancing commenced to take shape. The body once free, technical skill had its opportunity. Shortened skirts required the invention of new steps for the feet, now delivered from the clinging burden of long dresses. In 1730 Camargo discarded the heels on dancers' shoes, and was the first to introduce the *entrechat*, impossible on heels. Her *entrechats* were simple. They amounted to *four*, such as we term to-day the *entrechat quatre*. But in 1750 the *danseuse* Lany executed six, and even eight, a number never yet exceeded. It is rare if any one goes beyond six, for very few dancers accomplish seven—the *entrechat royale*.

In 1766 the *danseuse* Mlle. Heinel invented the *pirouette*, also, at first, quite simple, though it was to become more complicated later, when it was doubled, trebled, twirled *en dedans*. The dancers Gardel and Vestris brought in *ronds de jambe*; but it is unnecessary to follow the whole course of ballet virtuosity, which, under the control of the French school, continued to improve in style and interest. It was the Italian school that carried technique to doubtful extremes, inventing difficulties, imposing far-fetched and complicated methods, even transgressing the limits of the grotesque, of a positively inartistic style.

Noverre protested against this.

'Imagine,' he wrote, 'thirty dancers who execute during the ballet six pirouettes each in six circles. In a space of two or three hours they have made, altogether, 1,080 revolutions. But dervishes turn still quicker and execute a still greater number of revolutions; only nobody considers their whirling to be an art or the dervishes to be artists.'

The present writer once heard a Parisian 'star,' a very good classical dancer, say that, in a ballet, nothing mattered beyond technique and hard work. Serious work was not necessary. It only detracted from the ballet's value, by drawing the attention of the audience to other things and away from the dancing. To hear music, people must go to concerts, not to the ballet. As concerns the dance itself, '*La danse ce n'est autre chose que le travail*' ('Dancing means work, and nothing else!'). . . . These words were spoken in a drawing-room, the French people present listening to them as though they were a revelation.

Every art, to be effective, requires an impulse of the spirit, without which it becomes mere form; dull, soulless, and sometimes unbearably harsh. Yet even the Russian ballet, which, judging by its remarkable success, at least ought to have made a firm impression, if not an actual revolution, positively produced no effect on the methods of the French ballet. Doubtless, Parisian dancers admired the inspired execution of A. Pavlova and Karsavina, not to mention others of their country, who gave life and passion to every solo dance, every *ensemble* of such dances as those from *Prince Igor*, the *Bacchanale* and others; but the effect was imperceptible. Even now, the *danse travail* reigns on the French stage. The *figurante* has only to exhibit sufficient skill to please the Parisian connoisseur. He appears extraordinarily indifferent, even insen-

sible, to that artistry which informs the dancer if she is a musician as well.

Karsavina is the devoted exponent of the new dancing. Her art speaks to heart and to the imagination; but she is careful not to let the audience observe in it the celebrated *travail*, which she leaves somewhere behind the stage, in the academy, school or rehearsal room. The reason why her dancing is valuable is that, while it contains the labour, it is also inspired by life, passion and music.

At the beginning of her career, Karsavina, no doubt, lacked self-confidence; while a want of technique was noticeable in her classical dancing. She herself admits this in her *Recollections*. Again, in the desire to correct these blemishes, she strove hard to master what was required of her, until, by means of tireless endeavour, she acquired the needful virtuosity. Possessed of the knowledge that the highest form of art is the concealment of art, she has since forborne to parade her achievements in this respect. Probably that is why her dancing is so fascinating. It is because the grace, the music, the poetry and the precision in plastic design and choreographic movement that it contains are supported by a perfect technical skill that is not expressed and which, moreover, does not attract the eye. The spectator sees in her dancing only the plasticity of movement, the pose, the poetry and the imagination—and its fusion with the spirit of the period and the style of the composition.

Of all Karsavina's technical work the *pas de deux* in *Casse Noisette* is probably the most remarkable. Difficult though it is, it betrays neither strain nor effort, neither technical exaggeration nor inelegance of form and movement. It reigns supreme in its splendour of colouring and in what is termed the soul of classical dancing—rhythm. Not for a moment does the dancer seek to draw attention to such and such a detail, either of technique or colouring. Her pantomime is natural, unforced, lyrical . . . so also is her dancing. In her, fantasy and plasticity are one and indivisible.

A foreign critic has justly remarked of Karsavina that she has none of the 'star's' professional egoism on the stage. She does nothing for the mere sake of pleasing the audience or to gain applause. Her method is to lay aside feats of technique and to rely on form and rhythm.

During the latter part of her career, Karsavina's art has developed new and valuable forms. It has become thoughtful; her technique sounder, more complete. Since *Giselle*, *Chopiniana* and *Le Spectre de la Rose* her art is in the spirit of the present time, when dancing is free; when it can flower unhindered by tradition and prejudice; when it is no longer an acrobatic performance, leaping 'over and through' various articles. A spectator who admires artistic dancing, choregraphic expression, the embodiment of melody and rhythm in plastic motion, poses and attitudes that are delicate, graceful and pleasing, requires no analysis of the mechanical toil that a dancer has undergone behind and off the stage.

There will always be pedants, Philistines of technical classicism, who will seek to detect in every dancer something incomplete, something imperfect in the twirl of a *pirouette* or a faulty conclusion. These are amateurs in criticism, not *critics*. . . .

Karsavina's fame is European. She is an artist of choregraphic drama who has glorified the name and character of Russian art over all Europe and America. The world wishes her further success, further triumphs in the regions of Dance and Plastics. Some day the immortal Terpsichore will decree her a pleasant rest on the laurels acquired by her talents, but this day has not yet arrived. . . .

Karsavina's iconography is extensive and varied. It need not be detailed in the literary portion of this work. Great artists of almost every nationality have furnished her gallery with portraits of herself. The Anglo-Saxons, Filson, Lintott, Philpot and Sargent, have painted her; the French artists, G. Barbier, J. Blanche, de Thomas; the Russians, Eberling, Seroff, Sorin, Soudbinin; the Czech, Stretti; the Central Europeans, Borchardt, Kainer. Not only are there portraits of her, but portraits of her in her most famous *rôles*—*Fire-bird*, *Sylphide*, *Zobeide*, *Thamar*; portraits of her in society, at home; sketches of her dressing-rooms; her costumes—these in different ballets: *La Fille Mal Gardée* and *Midas*, by Douboujinsky; *The Tragedy of Salome*, by Soudeikine, etc. Oil-paintings, water-colours, pastels, paintings in tempera, have been made of her; drawings in pencil, charcoal, pen and ink; etchings. Engravings: *Karsavina at her Toilet*, by Duval; *Columbine*, engraving in colours. Statuettes in porcelain, silver and bronze by the *Imperial Porcelain Works* (Soudbinin); *Karsavina*, Hebrard's studio in Paris; *Karsavina*, statuette, Fredman-Clusel. . . .

Of literary works specially devoted to Karsavina there are several. Most of the books, pamphlets, albums, poems and reviews dedicated to her are not criticism; they are prose or poetry laid at the feet of the dancer. To take a few, such are the book *Karsavina dans ses Danses*, an album of water-colours by Georges Barbier, beautifully edited, with poems by Jean Vaudoyer; another book, *Karsavina*, published by the *Wandering Dog*, a writers' association, with cover by Soudeikine and poems by N. Kusmin, G. Ivanoff, N. Goumileff, A. Potiomkin, B. Sadovsky and others.

This collection of Russian writers may be suitably closed by a critical review by S. Stark, whose concluding sentences I transcribe:—' Remaining always and everywhere in the sphere of accomplished skill—which cannot be otherwise, because it is only through technique that the artist arrives at the revelation of all the secrets of beauty—Karsavina's dancing is like a sonnet, where every line is a gift to the altar of poetry. Her dancing is the flow of the stream, and not that of the angry sea. The lines of her dancing are simple and pure. Simplicity is the ennobling loveliness of Karsavina's creative work, as it is in every art. In this atmosphere bloom the most delicate flowers of the poetry of dancing, which the *ballerina*—like a fairy flying over woods, valleys, mountains and the sea—distributes to the world.

CAMERA PORTRAITS

Rôle of Giselle in Giselle
(Camera Portrait—Fischer)

Rôle of Zobeide in Schéhérazade
(*Camera Portrait—E. O. Hoppé*)

Rôle of Columbine in Le Carnaval
(*Camera Portrait—Sandru-Sellin*)

Rôle of Armide in Le Pavillon d'Armide
(Camera Portrait—E. O. Hoppé)

Rôle of The Queen of Shemâkhan in Le Coq d'Or
(*Camera Portrait—E. O. Hoppé*)

Rôle of Sylphide in Les Sylphides
(*Camera Portrait—Schneider*)

Rôle of The Young Girl in Papillons
(*Camera Portrait—Saul Bransburg*)

Rôle of The Maiden in Le Spectre de la Rose
(*Camera Portrait—Schneider*)

Rôle of Chloë in Daphnis et Chloë
(Camera Portrait—E. O. Hoppé)

Rôle of The Ballerine in Petrouchka
(*Camera Portrait—Schneider*)

Rôle of Salome in The Tragedy of Salome
(Camera Portrait—E. O. Hoppé)

Rôle of The Fire-Bird in L'Oiseau de Feu
(Camera Portrait—Bertram Park)

Rôle of The Miller's Wife in The Three Cornered Hat
(Camera Portrait—Malcolm Arbuthnot)

Rôle of Pimpinella in Pulcinella
(*Camera Portrait—E. O. Hoppé*)

Pas de Deux in Le Astuzie Femminili
(*Camera Portrait—E. O. Hoppé*)

BIBLIOGRAPHY

THAMAR KARSAVINA ou l'Heure dansante au Jardin du Roi. Texte de Robert Brussel. With six designs by Gir—the first hand coloured. (1) *L'Oiseau d'Or* (full-length), (2) *At Rehearsal*, (3) *Giselle*, (4) *L'Oiseau d'Or* (head), (5) *L'Oiseau d'Or* (head), (6) *Le Carnaval*. Edition limited to 500 copies. Large 4to. Grey wrappers. *Circa* 1910.

MUSICA.—Noël. Contains ' *Souvenirs d'Enfance*,' by Mlle. Karsavina. Pp. 261. Folio. Illustrated wrappers. December, 1912.

ALBUM DEDIÉ À TAMAR KARSAVINA par George Barbier et Jean-Louis Vaudoyer. Contains verses by Vaudoyer and 12 hand-coloured designs of the dancer in her various *rôles* by Barbier. Printed on hand-made paper. Edition limited to 500 copies. Large 4to. Biscuit-coloured wrappers with design in black and gold. Corrard. 1914.

KARSAVINA.—A volume published by the members of the writers' club ' The Wandering Dog.' Text in Russian. Appreciation and Poems by N. Evrenov, M. Kousmin, V. Zalensky, G. Ivanoff, N. Goumileff, Anna Achmatova, N. Losinsky, Potiomkin, V. Svetlov, E. Stark. With decorations by Soudeikine and reproductions of portraits by Sargent, Sorine, Seroff, Kainer and Soudeikine. Small 4to. Pale fawn wrappers with design in red and blue. March 26th, 1914.

RUSSKY BALET.—A volume devoted to four *ballerines* of the Mariynsky (Imperial Ballet) Theatre. Text in Russian.
1. *A. P. Pavlova*. Appreciations by Andrei Levinson, Oskar Bie and N. Georgevitch.
2. *M. F. Kshesinskaïa*. Appreciations by A. Pleshtshayev and Andrei Levinson.
3. *O. O. Preobrajenskaïa*, by N. Georgevitch and Andrei Levinson.
4. *T. P. Karsavina*. Appreciation by V. Svetlov.

Profusely illustrated with photographs throughout the text. Folio. Dark grey-green wrappers, lettered in gold. N.D.

THE BALLET RÉPERTOIRE OF THAMAR KARSAVINA

Name of Ballet.	Rôle.	Chorégraphe.	Designer of Costumes and Scenery.	Composer of Music.
Arlequinade	Columbine	Petipa	—	Drigo
Bayadère (La)	Variation in the 'Ghosts'	Petipa	—	Minkus
,,	Manu			
,,	Nikia			
Belle au Bois Dormant (La)	The Little White Cat	Petipa	—	Tchaikovsky
,,	The Fairy of the Lilacs			
,,	Aurore			
Boutique Fantasque (La)	A Can-Can Dancer	Massine	Derain	Rossini-Resphigi
Caprices du Papillon (Les)	Papillon	Petipa	—	—
Carnaval (Le)	Columbine	Fokine	Bakst	Schumann
Casse Noisette	Golden Waltz	Petipa	—	Tchaikovsky
,,	Fée Dragée			
Children's Tales (Contes Russes)	The Swan Queen	Massine	Gontcharova and Larionoff	Liadoff
Chopiniana (Les Sylphides)	Sylphide	Fokine	Benois [1]	Chopin
Coq d'Or (Le)	The Queen of Shemâkhan	Fokine	Gontcharova	Rimsky-Korsakoff

[1] There have been at least three scenes designed for this ballet. The first by A. Benois and two others respectively by Douboujinsky and Socrate.

Name of Ballet.	Rôle.	Chorégraphe.	Designer of Costumes and Scenery.	Composer of Music.
Corsaire (Le)	Medora	Petipa	—	Minkus
Daphnis et Chloë	Chloë	Fokine	Bakst	Ravel
Dieu Bleu (Le)	The Young Girl	Fokine	Bakst	Reynaldo Hahn
Don Quichotte	Kitri	Petipa	Golovine	Minkus
,,	The Flower Girl			
Eunice [1]	Actea	Fokine	—	—
,,	Eunice			
Fairy of the Dolls (The) (Puppen-Fée)	The Spanish Doll	Hastreit	Legat	Serge and Nicholas Bauer
,,	Fairy			
Festin (Le) [2]	Variation	Petipa	Korovine	Tchaikovsky
,,	L'Oiseau d'Or			
Fille du Pharaon (La)	The Fisher Girl	Petipa	—	Pugni
Fille Mal Gardée (La)	Lisa	Ivanoff	Douboujinsky	Hartel
Giselle, ou Les Willis	Giselle	Corali	Benois	Adams
Good Humoured Ladies (The)	Mariuccia	Massine	Bakst	Scarlatti-Tommasini
Graziella	Graziella	Ivanoff	—	—

[1] Fokine's first essay in the new form of ballet.
[2] *Vide* p. 94. Svetlov (V.) Le Ballet Contemporain :—' Le Festin était composé de manière interessante. Il s'ouvrait par la marche du Coq d'Or de Rimsky-Korsakoff; puis venaient : Lesghinka (Glinka), L'Oiseau d'Or (Tchaikovsky), Czardas (Glazounoff), Pas Classique hongrois (Glazounoff) et un Finale tiré de la deuxième symphonie de Tchaikovsky.'
The 'Programme des Representations au Théâtre National de l'Opéra' Saison des Ballets Russes, 1910, gives the composition of this ballet as follows :—I. Mazurka (Glinka); II. L'Oiseau d'Or; III. Hopak (Moussorgski); IV. Pas de Deux; V. Lesghinka (Rubinstein).

Name of Ballet.	Rôle.	Chorégraphe.	Designer of Costumes and Scenery.	Composer of Music.
In the Kingdom of Ice.	A Snowflake	Gerdt	—	T. C. and P. M.
Islamei	The Queen	Fokine	Anisfeld	Balakireff
Javotte	Pas de Deux	Petipa	—	Saint-Saëns
,,	'The Fisherman and the Pearl'[1]			
Jeux	A Maiden	Nijinsky	Bakst	Debussy
Kalkabrino	Variation[2]	Petipa	—	Drigo
Lac des Cygnes (Le)	Odetta-Odilia	Petipa	Korovine and Golovine	Tchaikovsky
,,	Variation			
Le Astuzie Femminili	Pas de Deux	Massine	Sert	Cimarosa-Resphigi
Légende de Joseph (La)	The Wife of Potiphar	Fokine	Sert and Bakst	Strauss
Little Red Flower (The)	The Rose	Legat	Korovine	Hartmann
Midas	Oréade	Fokine	Douboujinsky	Steinberg
Midnight Sun (The)	The Snow Maiden	Massine	Gontcharova and Larionoff	Rimsky-Korsakoff
Narcisse	Echo	Fokine	Bakst	Tcherepnine
Nuit d'Egypte (Une) (Cléopâtre)	Ta-Hor	Fokine	Bakst	Arensky

[1] A variation famous for its having been danced by Virginia Zucchi. It was an excerpt from the ballet *L'Ordre du Roi* (choregraphy by Petipa).
[2] Her partner was Lydia Kyasht.

Name of Ballet.	Rôle.	Chorégraphe.	Designer of Costumes and Scenery.	Composer of Music.
Oiseau de Feu	The Fire-Bird	Fokine	Bakst and Golovine	Stravinsky
Papillons	The Young Girl	Fokine	Bakst and Douboujinsky	Schumann
Paquita "	Paquita Pas de Trois [1]	Mazillier	—	Deldevèse
Parade	The American Girl	Massine	Picasso	Satie
Pavillon d'Armide (Le)	Armide	Fokine	Benois	Tcherepnine
Petit Cheval Bossu (Le) (Koniok Gorbounok) " "	Girl from Little Russia A Living Statue Tsar Vierge	St. Léon	—	Pugni
Petrouchka	The Ballerine	Fokine	Benois	Stravinsky
Pierrot's Dream	Columbine	Romanoff	—	Assaxieff
Préludes (Les)	A Human Soul	Fokine	Anisfeld	Liszt
Pulcinella	Pimpinella	Massine	Picasso	Pergolesi-Stravinsky
Raymonda " "	Pas Classique hongrois Variation 'Visions' Raymonda	Petipa	—	Glazounoff
Réveil de Flore (Le)	Flore	—	—	Drigo

[1] Her partners were A. Vaganova and N. G. Legat.

Name of Ballet.	Rôle.	Chorégraphe.	Designer of Costumes and Scenery.	Composer of Music.
Roxane . . .	Pas de Deux [1]	Petipa	—	—
Ruses d'Amour . .	Isabella	—	—	—
Saisons (Les) . .	The Snow Fairy	Petipa	Golovine	Glazounoff
Scheherazade . .	Zobeide	Fokine	Bakst	Rimsky-Korsakoff
Spectre de la Rose (Le)	The Maiden	Fokine	Bakst	Weber
Thamar . . .	Thamar	Fokine	Bakst	Balakireff
Three Cornered Hat (The) (Le Tricorne)	The Miller's Wife	Massine	Picasso	De Falla
Tragedy of Salome (The)	Salomé	Romanoff	Soudeikine	Florent Schmitt

[1] The first occasion on which Nijinsky was her partner.

INDEX OF NAMES, RÔLES AND BALLETS

ACTEA, 33, 35
AMOÛN, 63
Andersen, 56
Andrianoff, 12
Anisfeld, 90
Après-Midi d'un Faune (L'), 64, 66
AQUILON, 32
Arlequinade, 87, 97
ARMIDE, 7, 46, 49, 50, 51, 69, 89
Assaxieff, 88
AURORE, 71, 85, 86
Awakening (The) (in *Pierrot's Dream*), 88

Bacchanale, 100
Bakst, 3, 48, 50, 52
Balakireff, 61, 90
BALLERINE (THE) (in *Petrouchka*), 51, 55, 56
'Ballet Contemporain (Le),' by V. Svetlov, 38, 64
Ballet for Chopin's Music (*Chopiniana, Les Sylphides*), 34, 39, 46, 47, 48, 50, 63, 69, 88, 89, 97, 102
Ballet School (St. Petersburg and Imperial), 9, 11
Ballet School (Petrograd State), 9, 11
Barbier, 102, 103
BAYADÈRE (LA), 14, 28, 78, 79, 97
BEAUGENCY (RENÉ DE), 7
Beethoven, 55
Belle au Bois Dormant (La), 25, 31, 42, 70, 71, 83, 85
Benois (Alexander), 3, 46, 48, 51, 53, 56, 57
Beretta (Signora), 15, 16, 18
Berlin, 24
Bibliography, 137
Birbanto, 34
BIRD OF FIRE, 53, 70, 102
Blanche (J.), 102

Blasis (Carlo), 'History of Dancing,' quoted, 38
Borchardt, 102
Botticelli, 7, 91
Boucher, 46
Brusselle (Robert), 42, 43
Buda-Pesth, 25
BUDDHIST GIRL, 63, 64
Buenos Ayres, 66
Byron, 34, 35, 79

Calvocoressi (M. D.), 64 (footnote)
Camargo, 87, 96, 99
Caprices du Papillon (Les), 87
CARABOSSE, 25
Carnaval (Le), 39, 45, 47, 48, 50, 69, 89, 97
Casse Noisette, 14, 25, 70, 71, 83, 86, 101
Cecchetti (E.), 18, 19
Champs-Elysées (Théâtre des), 54
Chasse aux Alouettes (in *Arlequinade*), 87
Châtelet (Théâtre du), 42
Chinese Theatre (of Tsarkoe Selo), 11
CHLOË, 52
Chopin, 7, 34, 35, 46, 69
Chopiniana (*Ballet for Chopin's Music, Les Sylphides*), 34, 39, 46, 47, 48, 50, 63, 69, 88, 89, 97, 102
Clairon, 96
Cléopâtre (*Une Nuit d'Egypte*), 26, 34, 39, 62, 70, 76, 77, 88, 97
COLIN, 88
COLUMBINE (in *Arlequinade*), 87
COLUMBINE (in *Le Carnaval*), 7, 47, 59, 87, 102
COLUMBINE (in *Pierrot's Dream*), 88
Comedians' Rest, 91
Coppélia, 20
Coq d'Or (Le), 45, 53, 54

CORSAIR (LITTLE), 79, 80
Corsaire (Le), 34, 35, 70, 71, 79, 80, 83
Covent Garden (Theatre Royal), 44
Cygne (Le), 91

Daphnis et Chloë, 50, 52
Debussy, 3, 66
Delibes, 24, 80
Despreaux, 42
De Thomas, 102
'Deux Sonnets de l'Amoureux de Columbine (Les),' 47
Diaghileff (S. P.), 1, 3, 39, 42, 45, 52, 54, 64, 88
Didelot, 96
Dieu Bleu (Le), 63
Dobrovolskaïa, 55
Don Quichotte, 27, 28, 80
Douboujinsky, 3, 102
Dream (The) (in *Pierrot's Dream*), 88
Dresses worn in class (Colour of), 11
Drigo (R.), 22, 74, 82
Dukas, 3
Duncan (Isadora), 34, 50, 88
Duval, 102

Eberling, 102
ECHO, 5, 43, 50, 51, 52, 69, 97, 98
Eros, 88
Esmeralda, 20, 97
Eunice, 33, 34, 39, 50, 88, 89
EUNICE, 89

FAIRY (in *Konïok Gorbounok*), 71
FAIRY OF THE DOLLS (THE), 27, 87
FAIRY OF THE LILACS (THE), 31
FÉE DRAGÉE, 86
Fenella, 20, 97
Figaro, 42
Fille du Pharaon (La), 28, 96
Fille Mal Gardée (La), 20, 87, 96, 97, 102
Filson, 102
Finesse d'Amours, 79
Fisherman and the Pearl (The), 14
Fokine (Michel), 1, 3, 33, 34, 37, 38, 39, 46, 48, 50, 52, 61, 63, 64, 70, 74, 76, 83, 88, 89, 90, 91, 94

Fredman-Clusel, 103
French School of Dancing, 40

Gardel, 100
Gautier, 76
Geltzer, 29
Gerdt (P. A.), 11, 16
Germany, 44
Ghosts (in *La Bayadère*), 7, 14, 79
GIRL KING, 30, 32, 33, 53, 71, 82
GISELLE, 51, 97, 98
Giselle ou les Willis, 26, 75, 76, 77, 87, 96, 97, 98, 102, 104
Glazounoff, 3, 26, 28, 74, 86, 87
Golden Waltz (in *Casse Noisette*), 14
Gordon-Clifford, 44
Gorsky (A.), 80, 82
Grand Opéra (Paris), 44
Grand Opéra (St. Petersburg), 24
Grandmother's Tales, 24
Graziella, 26, 66
Grisi (C.), 97
Guimard, 96
Gumileff (N.), 103

Hartmann, 34
Hebrard, 103
Heinel, 99
Hellas, 5, 6, 43
'History of Dancing (The),' by C. Blasis, quoted, 38
Hoffmann, 25, 46

In the Kingdom of Ice, 11
Invitation à la Valse, 48
ISABELLA, 86, 87
Islamei, 39, 61, 63, 70, 74, 88, 89, 90, 97, 99
Italian School of Dancing, 40
IVAN THE TZAREVITCH, 53
Ivanoff (G.), 78, 103

Jardin Animé, 35, 80
Javotte, 14, 20
'Je sais tout,' 13
Jeux, 64, 65, 66
Johannsen, 15, 18

Kainer, 102
Kalkabrino, 31
KHAN'S WIFE, 70
KING DODON, 55
KING OF THE ALPINE ICE, 12
KING OF THE BLACK ISLANDS AND MOUNTAINS, 90
KITRI, 7, 27
Konïok Gorbounok (Le Petit Cheval Bossu), 29, 70, 71
KOSTCHEÏ, 54
Kousmin (N.), 103
Krachkovski (D.), 47
Kshesinskaïa (M. F.), 20, 23, 24, 29, 33, 85, 86, 97
Kulichevskaïa (R. M.), 11
Kyasht (Lydia), 12, 13, 31

Lac des Cygnes (Le), 11, 32, 33, 70, 71, 83, 84
Lamartine, 90, 91
Lany, 99
Legat (Brothers), 27
Legat (N. G.), 28
Legnani (Pierrina), 23, 29, 32, 72, 84, 85, 86, 93, 94, 95
Le Nôtre, 69
Lermontoff, 58
Liapounoff (S. M.), 90
Lintott, 102
LISE, 20, 88
Liszt (Franz), 47, 90, 91
LITTLE WHITE CAT (THE), 31, 35
Living Statues (in *Konïok Gorbounok*), 29
London, 3, 44, 66, 68
Longus, 52
Louis XIV., 46, 49, 59, 69

Maeterlinck, 56
MARCELLA, 16
Mariynsky Theatre, 12, 13, 14, 19, 31, 38, 44, 45, 61, 83, 88
MAZEPPA, 29
MEDORA, 34, 35, 79
Michel Theatre, 11
Midas, 52, 102
Milan, 15
Molli, 96

Monakhoff, 12
Monte Carlo, 44
MOOR (THE) (in *Petrouchka*), 56, 57

Narcisse, 5, 6, 39, 45, 50, 52, 69, 97
NARCISSE, 51, 98
Narodny Divaldo Theatre (Prague), 24, 25
Nedbal, 24, 25
Nereids, 30, 82
Nijinsky, 3, 24, 31, 32, 42, 48, 51, 56, 57, 64, 65, 66
NIKIA, 78, 79
Noverre, 100
Nuit d'Egypte (Une) (Cléopâtre), 26, 34, 39, 62, 70, 76, 77, 88, 97

Obukoff, 11
ODETTA-ODILIA, 32, 33, 35, 84
Oiseau de Feu, 42, 45, 53, 54, 70
Oiseau d'Or, 42

Palette, 47
PANADÉROS, 28
Papillons, 39, 48, 88, 89, 97
Paquerette, 66
Paquita, 27, 28, 70, 81
PAQUITA, 81
Paris, 39, 40, 41, 42, 43, 44, 47, 54, 66, 68
Pas classique hongrois, 29, 87
Pavillon d'Armide (Le), 39, 46, 88, 89
Pavlova (Anna), 10, 20, 23, 24, 27, 28, 33, 39, 75, 76, 78, 97, 98, 100
'Pélleas et Mélisande,' 66
Petipa (Marie), 28
Petipa (Marius), 19, 20, 33, 37, 38, 44, 45, 50, 64, 70, 71, 78, 83, 96
Petit Cheval Bossu (Le) (Konïok Gorbounok), 29, 30, 31, 32, 53, 82, 83, 70
Petrouchka, 39, 45, 51, 53, 55, 57
PETROUCHKA, 56
Philpot, 102
PIERROT (in *Papillons*), 89
Pierrot's Dream, 88, 89
'Poetical Meditations,' 90
Poisson d'Or (Le), 53, 82
Polovetz Dances (Prince Igor), 39, 100

Potiomkin (A.), 103
Poushkin, 13
Prague, 24, 26, 35
Prague Theatre (Narodny Divaldo), 24, 25
Preludes (Les), 7, 74, 88, 90, 99
Preobrajenskaïa (O. O.), 20, 24, 28, 29, 86
Prince Igor (*Polvetz Dances* from), 39, 100

Queen of Modern Dancing (The), 44
QUEEN OF SHEMÂKHAN, 54, 55

Ravel (M.), 52
Raymonda, 28, 29, 70, 86, 87
Recollections (of Karsavina), 13, 14, 15, 19, 21, 32, 38, 39, 40, 101
Red Flower (*The*), 34
Return from the Carnival (*The*) (in *Pierrot's Dream*), 88
Réveil de Flore (Le), 14, 22, 29, 32
Rimsky-Korsakoff, 54, 55, 90
Roehrich, 3
Romanoff, 3, 62, 74, 83, 88
ROSE (THE) (in *Les Saisons*), 86
Rose of Russia (The), 44
ROTBART, 7, 84
Roxane, 31
Rubinstein (Anton), 39
Ruses d'Amour, 26, 29, 86.
Rykliakova (V. T.), 14

Sacre de Printemps (Le), 64
Sadovsky, 103
Saint-Saëns, 91
Saisons (Les), 86
Sallé, 96
Salome (*The Tragedy of*), 62, 102
SALOME, 59
Sargent, 102
Schéhérazade, 6, 39, 43, 61, 63, 70, 90, 97
Schmitt (Florent), 62
Schollar (L.), 64, 65, 66
Schumann (Robert), 47, 69, 89
Sedova (T. A.), 11, 33
Seroff, 3, 102
Siegfried, 7

Skalkovsky (K. A.), 14, 22
SNOWFLAKES, 12
Sokolova (E. P.), 19
Sorin, 102
Soudbinin, 102, 103
Soudeikine, 3, 102, 103
Souroff, 3
South America, 44
SPANISH DOLL, 27, 28, 29
Spectre de la Rose (Le), 34, 35, 39, 43, 44, 45, 48, 63, 69, 97, 102
St. Leon, 19, 44, 78, 96
St. Petersburg, 18, 20, 26, 39, 44, 45, 47, 61, 68, 78, 80, 81, 88
St. Petersburg (Imperial School of), 9, 11
Stark (E.), 103
Steinberg, 52
Stepanko, 24
Stravinsky, 3, 42, 53
Stream (*The*), 28, 29
Stretti, 102
SVANILDA, 20
Svetlov (V.), ' Le Ballet Contemporain,' 38, 64
SYLPHIDE, 59, 60, 89, 102
Sylphides (Les) (*Chopiniana, Ballet for Chopin's Music*), 34, 39, 46, 47, 48, 50, 63, 69, 88, 89, 97, 102
Sylvie, 24

Taglioni (M.), 20, 34, 48, 93
TA-HOR, 7, 62, 70, 77
Tchaikovsky, 25, 32, 42, 74, 82, 83, 86
Tcherepnine, 3, 50, 89
Teliakovsky (V. A.), 9, 24
Thamar, 70
THAMAR (QUEEN), 61, 70, 102
Theatres :—
    London : Theatre Royal, Covent Garden, 44
    Paris : Grand Opéra, 44 ; Théâtre des Champs-Élysées, 54 ; Théâtre du Châtelet, 42
    Prague : Narodny Divaldo Theatre, 24, 25
    St. Petersburg : Grand Opéra, 24 ; Mariynsky Theatre, 12, 13, 14, 19, 31, 38, 44, 45, 61, 83, 88

'Thousand and One Nights,' 90
Tragedy of Salome (The), 102
Travelling Dancer (The), 29
Trefilova (V. A.), 14, 20, 28, 33
Triomphe de l'Amour (Le), 96
Tutchev, 58

Vaganova (A.), 28
Vaudoyer, 103
Vestris, 100
Vienna, 25
Vine (The), 39
Viscussi, 25
Visions (in *Raymonda*), 28

Vroubel, 70
Vsevolojsky (T. A.), 9, 24

'Wandering Dog (The),' 91, 103
Watteau, 46, 86
Weber, 48
Wieck (Clara), 47

YOUNG GIRL, 48
YOUNG HUNTER, 12

ZOBEIDE, 60, 70, 102
Zucchi (Virginia), 14, 23, 97

www.ingramcontent.com/pod-product-compliance
Lightning Source LLC
Chambersburg PA
CBHW060506240426
43661CB00007B/939